TRAFFICKING RHETORIC

NEW DIRECTIONS IN RHETORIC AND MATERIALITY
Wendy S. Hesford, Christa Teston, and Shui-Yin Sharon Yam, Series Editors

TRAFFICKING RHETORIC

RACE, MIGRATION, AND THE MAKING OF MODERN-DAY SLAVERY

Annie Hill

THE OHIO STATE UNIVERSITY PRESS

COLUMBUS

Library of Congress Cataloging-in-Publication Data

Names: Hill, Annie (Assistant Professor, Department of Rhetoric and Writing), author.

Title: Trafficking rhetoric : race, migration, and the making of modern-day slavery / Annie Hill.

Other titles: New directions in rhetoric and materiality.

Description: Columbus : The Ohio State University, [2024] | Series: New directions in rhetoric and materiality | Includes bibliographical references and index. | Summary: "A critical examination of the UK's antitrafficking agenda that exposes—through analysis of official estimates, policy papers, NGO reports, news stories, and awareness campaigns—the state's rescue mission as actually being an anti-immigration project intended to preserve the UK as an Anglo-white space"—Provided by publisher.

Identifiers: L CCN 2 023057111 | I SBN 9 780814215586 (hardback) | I SBN 0 814215580 (hardback) | ISBN 9780814283479 (ebook) | ISBN 0814283470 (ebook)

Subjects: LCSH: Human trafficking—Great Br itain. | Sl avery—Great Br itain. | Ra cism—Great Britain. | Rhetoric—Social aspects.

Classification: LCC HQ281 .H55 2024 | DDC 364.15/510941—dc23/eng/20240307

LC record available at https://lccn.loc.gov/2023057111

Other identifiers: ISBN 9780814259092 (paperback) | ISBN 081425909X (paperback)

Cover design by Alexa Love
Text composition by Stuart Rodriguez
Type set in Minion Pro

CONTENTS

ILLUSTRATIONS

ACKNOWLEDGMENTS

Many people and places offered me support and shelter during the decade it took to complete this book. I often cannot believe my good fortune and how the immense gift of my education put me in proximity to such incredible minds and generous souls. I hope my acknowledgments go some way in recognizing just how pivotal each step in this winding road has been.

As the only Black child in a Catholic grade school, I developed an early ambivalence to education. Mocked by students and underestimated by teachers, I sought alternative outlets for my interests as soon as I could, and I spent most of my teens working and volunteering at AIDS advocacy and environmental groups. I did not see education as a vehicle for political action but as something to sacrifice to effect social transformation. A high school counselor nominated me for a scholarship to the Community College of Philadelphia; that unexpected opportunity set me on this journey. Thank you so much, Mrs. Garfield and Principal Ellen Savitz, for not accepting the limits placed on working-class, poor, queer, Black and brown kids and for seeing us as stars.

At CCP I found a critical educational space unlike any I had known—one that provided a productive forum to merge my political and academic work. I witnessed how what I was learning sharpened my arguments about housing discrimination experienced by people living with AIDS and illness clusters linked to environmental racism. The merger of political action and academic inquiry, or *praxis*—the lived practice of ideas, the embodiment of theory—is the most significant concept I discovered. Thanks to the faculty in the CCP Honors Program for sparking my love of theory and inspiring me to pursue a bachelors degree. As a transfer student to Mount Holyoke College, I was incredibly lucky to find myself in the classrooms of Karen Barad and Joan Cocks. I am deeply grateful for their guidance, kindness, and boundless belief in me. It made me believe too.

At the University of California, Berkeley, Marianne Constable, Wendy Brown, Loïc Wacquant, and Samera Esmeir supervised my doctoral work and offered invaluable insights into the nascent project and, as important, the academic profession. Marianne was a rigorous graduate mentor and a lifeline when I experienced sexual harassment in my first academic job. Likewise, Wendy was quick to offer help and career-saving advice. I am here still because they were there then. I hope their influence is reflected in my pedagogy and professionalism for all of my career and that I never forget the critical lesson to *phone a feminist* when serious guidance is needed. At Berkeley, I benefitted immensely from being in community with Judith Butler, Daniel Boyarin, Pheng Cheah, David Cohen, Carol Clover, Trinh Minh-ha, and Sabrina Soracco. Fellow grads—Swati Rana, Sarah Wells, Sonali Thakkar, Sarah Reckhow, Yves Winter, Annika Thiem, Diana Anders—made my time at Cal less daunting and more thrilling.

At the University of Minnesota, Twin Cities, I am grateful to the Department of Gender, Women, and Sexuality Studies for offering me sanctuary. I learned critical feminist strategies for working and living from my passionate, courageous, and strong colleagues: Jigna Desai, Aren Z. Aizura, Lorena Muñoz, Siri Suh, Richa Nagar, Zenzele Isoke, and Naomi Scheman. Thanks also to Angelica Afanador-Pujol, Elliott Powell, Bianet Castellanos, Kevin Murphy, Jennifer Pierce, and David Valentine for enhancing my community at UMN. I offer deep gratitude especially to Catherine Squires for being a fierce advocate, ethical human, and brilliant thinker.

At the University of Texas at Austin, I have found a home (unless this red state makes it impossible to live here). For now, I get to work at my dream job in the Department of Rhetoric and Writing with great colleagues and endless sunshine. Thank you to the fine minds in DRW and affiliate spaces: Diane Davis, Scott Graham, Jo Hsu, Jackie Rhodes, Casey Boyle, Donnie Sackey, Mark Longaker, Clay Spinuzzi, Linda Ferreira-Buckley, Rasha Diab, Karma Chávez, Stacey Sowards, Alison Kafer, Lisa Moore, Cherise Smith, and so many others who make UT a good place. Also, I wish to offer a special note of thanks to the following scholars who enriched my professional life at crucial moments: Karma Chávez, Lisa Flores, Stacey Sowards, Catherine

Squires, Regina Kunzel, Dara Strolovitch, Jennifer Suchland, Wendy Hesford, Alison Kafer, Adela Licona, Bryan McCann, Ashley Mack, Leslie Harris, Rob Asen, Dan Brouwer, Mary Stuckey, Faber McAlister, Samantha Majic, Lauren McCarthy, Kirt Wilson, Cate Palczewski, Jiyeon Kang, Belinda Stillion-Southard, Isaac West, Damien Pfister, Jeff Bennett, Kari Vasby Anderson, and Angela Ray. Thank you for your advice, community, and encouraging words.

An amazing group of people helped to make this book become a real thing in the world. My heartfelt gratitude to Karma Chávez, Lisa Flores, and Stacey Sowards for keen feedback on the entire manuscript and loving impatience with my perfectionism. Thank you to Julietta Hua, Lauren Martin, Jennifer Suchland, Scott Graham, and Jo Hsu for offering generative comments on individual chapters. A sincere shout-out to Anjali Vats for her astute and generous response to my Public Address Conference plenary. I also presented parts of the book at venues including The Ohio State University, the University of Arizona, Drake University, the Program in Gender and Sexuality at Princeton, the Women's Studies Research Center at Mount Holyoke College in the Five College Consortium, the Institute for Advanced Studies at the University of Minnesota, and the Women's and Gender Studies Faculty Development Program at the University of Texas. Cheers to everyone who asked tough questions and helped to push the project forward! For first-rate editorial and indexing services, thanks to Ideas on Fire and to Morgan Blue, and to Kate Epstein for eagle-eyed attention to my work. I had hoped to put my first book in good hands, and Tara Cyphers, the anonymous readers, and the series editors exceeded all expectations. I am grateful for Tara's clarity and confidence in this project, and her enduring faith that I would get it done.

An earlier version of chapter 2 appeared as "The Rhetoric of Modern-Day Slavery: Analogical Links and Historical Kinks in the United Kingdom's Anti-Trafficking Plan," *PhiloSOPHIA: A Journal of Continental Feminism* 7, no. 2 (2017): 55–83.

Work of this kind needs sustained support, and I found funds, spaces, interlocutors, and friends across the US and UK as I pursued the shifting shapes of this project. I am indebted to the University of Cambridge's Institute of Criminology for sharing amazing resources—and Loraine Gelsthorpe was a gracious and inspiring host at Pembroke College, where I had a fantastic time. Berkeley's Center for British Studies got me to Cambridge through its exchange program. The Empirical Legal Studies Fellowship from Berkeley's Center for the Study of Law and Society helped me to complete the doctorate. A Ford Foundation postdoctoral fellowship facilitated a pivotal turn in my career, and for that, I will always be grateful. Thanks to Carrie Baker for being my sponsor at Smith College. The Office of the Vice President for Research at the University of Texas gave support as I finished the book during the COVID-19 pandemic. It's been a journey.

I will close by thanking those who have been my dearest fellow-travelers. My love and gratitude to Ian Junker, Maryanne DiPerri, Marissa Josephick, Leslie Simon, Meşve Vardar and, for those surreal years in France, un bisou aux filles, Nell Derick Debevoise, Oriana Reid-Collins, Brook Machin, and Mary Welsh. To Oscar and Charlie for being the most anarchic and cuddly dogs on earth, and to the feral farm for making the garden into a cat-centric and calming place. To Paul J. Junker Jr., thank you for the unconditional love, unending support, and for defending me and my life. I love you. To Rosemarie A. Hill, the woman who gave me life and taught me how to live it, I dedicate this book and everything I do. And to Karma, perfectly named, you are a fantasy made real, a gift from a ghost, and a political, intellectual, and ethical guide for making this life deeper and sweeter than I ever could have imagined. We wanted more and we got it, my love.

The Torque of State Veneration and State Violence

On June 7, 2020, during global protests after the police murder of George Floyd, Black Lives Matter (BLM) protesters in Bristol toppled an eight-foot bronze statue of English slave trader Edward Colston. Before being dragged to the docks of Bristol Harbour, the face and chest of the statue had been sprayed with red paint. The paint symbolized the bloodshed of the transatlantic slave trade but also evoked the Royal African Company's practice of branding its initials into the chests of enslaved adults and children.

King Charles II established the Royal African Company (RAC) with his brother, who was its formal head and later ascended the throne as James II. Between 1672 and 1689, the RAC dominated the West African slave trade and transported more people than any other company in the entire history of the transatlantic trade. Thus, what Great Britain would become was built on a triangular trade that forcibly transported Africans to the Americas and Caribbean, and the crops that they were compelled to tend traveled to Britain and beyond, thereby generating two revenue streams for the British Empire.

Edward Colston served as an RAC official from 1680 to 1692, a period during which the RAC shipped an estimated 84,000 Africans, more than 20,000 of whom are thought to have died en route. The living were tightly packed onto ships to ensure optimal profits for each voyage, and those killed by the lethal conditions onboard were dumped at sea. The violence and brutality of

FIGURE 1. Edward Colston statue in Bristol,
UK. Used with permission from Alamy.

the slave trade cannot be overstated, but still the statue of Colston stood, chin in hand, gazing over one of the most diverse cities in the United Kingdom (see figure 1).

The Colston statue had drawn public controversy for decades, with campaigns to get the city to remove it or to revise its commemorative plaque, which read: "Erected by citizens of Bristol as a memorial of one of the most virtuous and wise sons of their city." The statue was erected in 1895 to commemorate Colston's philanthropy in Bristol. A revised plaque would at least say that the slave trade contributed to the fortune amassed by Colston. The lord mayor of Bristol vetoed a revision to the plaque, however, and the city council refused to remove the statue. In response to the intransigence, BLM protesters toppled this symbol of not only a slave trader but a city's veneration of that slave trader. Some local politicians applauded the statue's fall. Labour MP for Bristol West, Thangam Debbonaire, reflected, "Having statues of people who oppressed us is not a good thing to be saying to black people in this city."[1] Statuary was not the only thing sending a celebratory message about

---

1. Siddique and Skopeliti, "BLM Protesters Topple Statue."

Colston. His statue stood on Colston Avenue. The city's largest music hall was called Colston Hall before a name change in 2017, its site originally a boarding school for boys founded by Colston in 1710. For centuries, Bristol has been marked by buildings, roads, monuments, and even a sweet bun named after Colston, which the Colston Society distributed to children on Colston Day. And yet, Edward Colston had trafficked humans on a staggering scale.

As I read the transatlantic news about Colston's fall and watched videos of the crowd cheering while the statue sank underwater, I remembered living in Bristol and in Minneapolis. I call this news "transatlantic" because Colston's fall also signals something for the United States and how it commemorates enslavers. Both Bristol and Minneapolis influenced the course of my life. In my twenties, I worked as a bartender at a pub in Bristol City Centre, a few streets away from the Colston statue. I saw the statue as one of many rhetorical and material reminders that Bristol had been a major English port in the slave trade. Other reminders included Guinea Street, Queen Square, Bristol's first banks, and the Old Vic (one of Europe's oldest theaters), all funded by city sons reaping slavery's rewards. The Colston statue appeared to be a fixture in a city that materialized through the immense profits made from a traffic in people.

In my thirties while living in Minneapolis, my buses home from work connected at 38th Street and Chicago Avenue. At this crossroads, on May 25, 2020, a police officer killed George Floyd in a public display of torture that philosopher Michel Foucault declared had disappeared with the advent of modern penal codes. The racist state violence inflicted on Floyd was the latest in a litany of killings caught on camera and receiving global media coverage that documented US law enforcement murders of Black adults and children, often in broad daylight and public view. This particular murder by Minneapolis police sparked national and international protests *against* racist state violence and *for* Black lives.

Weeks before the toppling of the Colston statue, mainstream and social media circulated cell phone video of Floyd's murder, in the wake of a 911 call by a store clerk who suspected him of passing a bogus twenty-dollar bill. Anti-Black violence, and centuries-long resistance to that violence, are part of the struggle over state racism, the devaluation and destruction of Black life, and the terror and tenacity of white supremacy. We live in a world in which a statue of a slave trader stands for more than a century, and a police officer kneels on a Black man's neck for nine lethal minutes ostensibly over counterfeit coin. Given existing conditions, I argue in *Trafficking Rhetoric* that the torque of state veneration and state violence is evinced—it is evidenced— when a state points to the supposed misdeeds of others as a way of celebrating itself and concealing its own aggression. For instance, take the foreword to the 2007 *UK Action Plan on Tackling Human Trafficking*, which reads:

> This year, it is 200 years since Parliament passed the Act to abolish the slave trade in the British Empire. Whilst we reflect on the past with the numerous events planned to mark the bicentenary, we must not forget the plight of the thousands of people who are still forced to live in slave like conditions as a result of the inhuman criminal practices perpetrated by 21st century traffickers.[2]

In this excerpt, the UK government venerates abolition in order to authorize state action against "21st century traffickers," who, it memorably explains, engage in "inhuman criminal practices." There is no mention of the legislative acts by which the British Crown supported the slave trade and gave charters to companies supplying enslaved people to the colonies and advancing British interests in Africa. Of course, the transatlantic slave trade had not been defined as a crime then, because the British Empire enshrined it in law, producing legislation to justify and protect its investment in human bondage. That trade in human beings was an explicitly national and legal enterprise for Britain, but human trafficking in the twenty-first century is to be understood as an illegal racket named *modern-day slavery*. The only past the *Action Plan* foreword acknowledges is abolition, which it links to the antitrafficking agenda. My initial reaction was incredulity when witnessing the UK's rhetorical deployment and disavowal of the transatlantic slave trade through the torque of state veneration and state violence.

I first encountered trafficking rhetoric while working in the UK again in 2007, no longer a bartender in Bristol but a graduate student studying criminology. At that time, the bicentennial celebration of abolition was in full swing, and I heard government officials invoking abolition as the precedent for the national plan to tackle human trafficking. They told a triumphant tale about Britain abolishing the transatlantic slave trade and reviving that righteous battle now that human trafficking had arrived on British soil. Circulating salacious stories about sex slaves, mainstream and tabloid media amplified the government's *modern-day slavery* rhetoric, thereby analogizing human trafficking with historical slavery.

Trafficking Rhetoric chronicles that, in the year 2007 alone, the UK government unveiled a national antitrafficking plan, public awareness campaign, unprecedented police operation, and £2 coin to commemorate abolition, with Queen Elizabeth II on one side and a broken manacle on the other. Note how the UK was venerating slave traders (Colston statue) and abolition (£2 coin) simultaneously, and seamlessly too. The government articulated a hagiography

---

2. Home Office, *UK Action Plan*, 2.

about abolition to promote a hostile environment for "21st century traffickers" while targeting irregular migrants, sex workers, and minority citizens. The UK antitrafficking agenda raises interrelated questions: How did the government use trafficking rhetoric to represent Britain as an abolitionist nation but also to suppress unsettled debts to the descendants of enslaved people? What kinds of knowledge and expertise validated trafficking estimates, law and policy, and police operations? Why did the contemporary struggles over migration, race, labor, and nation both revive and bury histories of slavery, imperialism, and colonialism? To begin addressing these questions, *Trafficking Rhetoric* analyzes how the transatlantic slave trade was remembered and forgotten as the United Kingdom embarked on a new national enterprise: the battle against twenty-first-century trafficking.

MATERIALS AND METHODS

To investigate the UK's antitrafficking agenda, I study major sites of its rhetorical and material invention including official estimates, policy papers, laws, NGO reports, news stories, and public awareness materials. Although some commentators have dismissed antitrafficking agendas as merely rhetorical, thereby setting up a conceptual framework that contrasts mere rhetoric with material reality, the rhetorical criticism that I perform in this book starts from the premise that *rhetoric is material*. I thus handle trafficking texts as material rhetoric, grasping "the material and discursive as co-constitutive," rather than as separate elements or as existing in opposition.[3] Handling material rhetoric shows how "discourse produces the issue under consideration in the first place—shaping how the problem is defined, how it can be perceived, and the possible moral and political responses that can emerge."[4] It elucidates what trafficking texts do *in* the world *as* world-making matter. Feminist theorist and physicist Karen Barad writes, "Meaning is not an ideality; meaning is material. And matter isn't what exists separately from meaning. Mattering is a matter of what comes to matter and what doesn't."[5] Central to this book, then, is explicating why and how trafficking rhetoric came to matter in the UK.

To that end, I focus mostly on trafficking texts that appeared before the UK captured and processed the people it would point to as evidence, or material referents, for trafficking. A lack of visible victims and perpetrators put pressure on the UK to find trafficked women and children, and the men it

---

3. Hesford, *Violent Exceptions,* 22.
4. Bernstein, *Brokered Subjects,* 28.
5. Barad, "Diffracting Diffraction," 175.

claimed were trafficking them. Investigating the gaps between trafficking rhetoric and bodily referents, I argue that trafficking is not a thing the state can simply seek and find, nor is it a linguistic construction conjured out of whole cloth. Rather, state apparatuses, like the UK Human Trafficking Centre and the UK Border Agency, conscript people as state agents, vigilant citizens, advocates, antitrafficking professionals, trafficking victims, and perpetrators to flesh out this state venture, which cannot be evaluated only in terms of rational decision-making and data-driven governance. To understand how antitrafficking was turned into a national project, the UK must be situated within the larger EU context and within histories of Britain's oscillating use of enslavement, forced migration, and immigration control. By tracking how the antitrafficking and anti-immigration agendas coalesced in the early twenty-first century, I foreground the possessive nationalism that claims the UK as white space, specifically as an Anglo-white nation.

Trafficking Rhetoric focuses on the UK's articulation of trafficking from its emergence as a state concern to the historic vote that led the UK to exit the EU. Using genealogical methods, I track the UK antitrafficking agenda from 2000 to 2022, paying close attention to 2007, a pivotal year in its construction. As critical rhetoric and human rights scholar Wendy S. Hesford affirms, one strength of genealogical methods is that they "draw attention to how history is narrated and mobilized to serve particular disciplinary and political agendas."[6] The UK government said that immigration restrictions and antitrafficking raids were rational reactions to forced migration and sexual exploitation. Border and crime control measures were couched as humanitarian missions justified by the sudden exigency to stop trafficking and save women and children. Paternalistic, racialized, and nationalist, the antitrafficking agenda unleashed state action against migrants and minority citizens, especially people working in the sex industry, while obscuring the violence of arrest, detention, deportation, and incarceration. Raids became recoded as rescue operations, and people held in detention were declared freed from slavery.

HISTORICAL SITES OF EXPANSION: UNITED KINGDOM / EUROPEAN UNION

The European Union experienced its largest expansion when ten countries acceded in 2004. Of the new members, Cyprus and Malta were already part of the Commonwealth, so their citizens had fewer entry restrictions to the UK.

---

6. Hesford, *Violent Exceptions,* 24.

The other new members were Poland, Slovenia, Slovakia, Hungary, Estonia, Lithuania, Latvia, and the Czech Republic, which were dubbed the Accession 8 (A8). Their postcommunist status and per capita incomes caused concern that accession would trigger mass migration to wealthy countries in the West.[7] Discussion of the A8 illustrates how an entire region can be turned into short-hand for economic migration. For example, BBC News circulated stereotypes about A8 migrants when declaring, "Everyone's heard about their friends who have just had the Polish plumber in to fix up the bathroom or been served a latte by a Latvian on their way to work."[8] The tropes of the Polish plumber and Latvian server convey the stereotypical story of migrant workers proliferating in the UK. Alongside poor but respectable migrants, so the story goes, traf-fickers are also taking advantage of EU enlargement. Xenophobic rhetoric, always already linked to immigration from Africa, Asia, and former British colonies, insinuates that East Europeans are counterfeit and cunning, on the move to exploit the UK's soft borders.

The early twenty-first century was not the first time that xenophobic tropes stigmatized East Europeans in Britain. A deep history of hostility directed the discursive flow engulfing East Europeans after EU enlargement. In this con-text, the term *Eastern European* names a racialized group linked with trans-national crime and economic migration. The term amalgamates people from diverse cultures and countries who are variously cast together as desirable or undesirable arrivals. Stigmatizing signifiers cohere what are often thought to be distinct groups. Feminist theorist Sara Ahmed posits that fear travels via the association of discursive figures, such as the migrant and the asylum seeker, engendering a belief that "any incoming bodies could be bogus, such that their 'endless' arrival is anticipated as a scene of 'our injury.'"[9] Through that fear, the "ordinary or normative subject is reproduced as the injured party: the one 'hurt' or even damaged by the 'invasion' of others."[10] Migrants appear as frightening figures causing harm to ordinary British citizens, who are, by contrast, represented as inhabiting and inheriting a superior but also victimized culture and country. The construction "of Britishness through whiteness," geographer Amy Clarke explains, "was also classed, facilitating the exclusion of working-class people, Jews, Irish, and other 'off-white' migrants,"

---

7. BBC News, "Who Are the 'A8 Countries?'" The "who" in the headline hints at a pre-occupation with the people migrating, rather than with the countries. The subtext of stories about A8 citizens migrating for work is an accusation that they lower wages and steal jobs from British workers.

8. BBC News, "Who Are the 'A8 countries?'"

9. Ahmed, "Affective Economies," 123.

10. Ahmed, "Affective Economies," 118.

in addition to the barriers against nonwhite migrants.[11] She contends that "a connection between Britishness and whiteness continues to be reproduced in the discursive construction of Britain as a nation rather than an empire and as ethnically homogenous pre-1945."[12] Feelings of fear and figures like traffickers fuel a possessive nationalism that paints Britain as diminished and ripped off by immigration it does not want.

British immigration policy since World War II has deemed people as racially desirable or undesirable. According to Fox and colleagues, "In the late 1940s, displaced East Europeans were recruited through the European Volunteer Worker scheme because of their racial suitability, although even here care was taken not to cast the net so widely as to include Jews."[13] The Immigration Acts of 1961 and 1962 obstructed the arrival of Black and brown citizens from Commonwealth countries as the UK "opened a backdoor to the Irish by exempting them from immigration control (despite the fact that they were neither citizens of the UK nor subjects of the Commonwealth)."[14] This is an instance of comparative racialization wherein Irish people, who had been excluded as inferior to Britons, became included by 1960s immigration policy when the UK decided that the Irish were preferable to Black and brown Commonwealth citizens. Shifting laws and policies index how migrant legal status is contingently ascribed by governments based on economic, social, racial, religious, and historical factors, among others. Legal status does not name essential human traits of goodness or badness, although state acts of exclusion arrive with xenophobic and racial rhetoric as justification. For instance, rhetoric scholarship is engaged in a vigorous conversation about US bordering practices, focusing on racial and immigration rhetoric that delineates included and excluded groups.[15]

Building on rhetoric scholarship and extending beyond its US focus, *Trafficking Rhetoric* examines the construction and positioning of East European whiteness against British whiteness in a geopolitical context of unstable financial markets and rapid EU expansion. The UK opened its door to East Europe in 2004 when "the European Union expanded significantly in terms of member states—from 15 to 25—and in population—to more than 500 million people (an increase of 28 per cent)," but the UK changed course when the

---

11. Clarke, "Recognising British Bodies," 3.
12. Clarke, "Recognising British Bodies," 3.
13. Fox, Moroşanu, and Szilassy, "Racialization," 683.
14. Fox, Moroşanu, and Szilassy, "Racialization," 683.
15. See, for example, Cisneros, *Border Crossed Us*; Flores, *Deportable and Disposable*; Chávez, *Queer Migration Politics*; DeChaine, *Border Rhetorics*; Chávez, *Borders of AIDS*; and Fixmer-Oraiz, *Homeland Maternity*.

EU's fifth enlargement included Romania and Bulgaria in 2007.[16] This oscillation on immigration marks a turn from the postwar era, when Britain desperately needed to rebuild the country and replenish labor markets and thus saw East European workers as desirable arrivals. Consequently, *Trafficking Rhetoric* contributes to scholarship that investigates the historical and ongoing incorporation of East Europeans in the UK by tracing how the antitrafficking agenda defines people who migrate, frames border control, and, above all, relies on state regimes of racialization.

The Home Office, which is the UK government department responsible for immigration and national security, published a report in 2003 estimating that net migration from the ten new EU members would range from 5,000 to 13,000 individuals annually up to the year 2010.[17] It stated, "even in the worst case scenario, migration to the UK as a result of Eastern enlargement of the EU is not likely to be overly large."[18] The report had a crucial caveat, however; it noted net migration to the UK would be higher if the labor markets of other EU states stayed closed. As it happened, only the UK, the Republic of Ireland, and Sweden opened their labor markets to new members. Shattering the earlier estimate, the UK Office for National Statistics later put the numbers from A8 states at 76,000 arrivals in 2005, 92,000 in 2006, and 112,000 in 2007.[19] But, citing its earlier incorrect estimate, the Labour government maintained that EU migration would be insignificant! As Fox and colleagues explain, the "robust British economy combined with the free market agenda of New Labour made the UK a good candidate for the influx of cheap labour from the East" in the early 2000s.[20] While migration flourished, the UK Independence Party, the Conservatives, the Liberal Democrats, and other rival parties accused Labour of losing control of British borders. Amid the political outcry, fear about transnational crime grew into a panic about the trafficking of East European women into the UK. The Great Recession struck when Romania and Bulgaria joined the EU, further impacting labor markets and public feelings about migrants.

The conceptual link between transatlantic slavery and human trafficking had been forged by 2007. The Labour government avowed its commitment to rescue modern-day slaves and root out traffickers. Meanwhile, it gave Romanians and Bulgarians (A2 migrants) "exclusive access to certain low-skilled schemes that had previously been the reserve of non-EU workers," thereby

16. McDowell, "Old and New European Economic Migrants," 19.
17. Dustmann et al., *Impact of EU Enlargement,* 57.
18. Dustmann et al., *Impact of EU Enlargement,* 57.
19. BBC News, "Labour's EU Migrant Policy."
20. Fox, Moroşanu, and Szilassy, "Racialization," 682.

directing them into industries with known exploitative practices and producing tiers of white EU migrants (A8 compared to A2).[21] The government simultaneously permitted and put restrictions on East Europeans' immigration for work, while using access to this labor pool to close the door on non-EU and nonwhite workers. The flexible racialization of UK immigration control indexes how borders materialize to govern human bodies, labor, and movement. Put another way, people do not cross the same border, because borders materialize differently across and through bodies. I intend to complicate and contribute to border rhetoric scholarship arguing that the border produces and manages difference but leaving in place a singular national border (e.g., "the border crossed us"). I track the rhetorical-material entanglements of borders and bodies to grasp the co-constitutive formations and divisions of "the border" and "us."

Along with tiered access to its labor market, the UK also created a category of exception: the *victim of trafficking*. The category signified "good migrant" status in contrast with *economic migrant, asylum seeker,* and *refugee,* which were framed as suspicious categories ripe for abuse by people trying to subvert immigration control. In this manner, the UK cast itself as victimized by migrants, including East Europeans with the right to migrate to the UK for work. Witness the torque of this tactic. The UK renders migrants as illegal and then creates an exceptional category of legal protection for a select group of migrants, to help them escape the effects of illegalization. At the same time, the UK's liberalization of migration policies to bring in cheap labor "has gone together with reassurances that the government will crack down hard on the 'villains,' not just 'bogus asylum seekers' but also 'illegal immigrants,' 'traffickers' and others seeking to abuse the system."[22] People put in separate categories encounter similar barriers: exclusion from entry and deportation upon discovery. A perception that *East European woman* meant *victim of trafficking* defined women from this region, who were forced to negotiate the conjoined stigmas of sex work and sex slavery. The white slavery panic of the late eighteenth and early nineteenth centuries, with its ribald tales of English women spirited away to brothels in Europe and South America, provided the discursive precedent for imagining slavery as something that befell white women.[23]

---

21. Fox, Moroşanu, and Szilassy, "Racialization," 685. While UK work restrictions on A8 and A2 migrants differed, each cohort was used to fill gaps in agriculture and food processing industries.

22. Anderson and Rogaly, "Forced Labour and Migration to the UK," 7.

23. For detail on the similarities between human trafficking and white slavery panics, see Doezema, *Sex Slaves and Discourse Masters*; Devereux, "'Maiden Tribute'"; and Harris, *Rhetoric of White Slavery.*

Notably, trafficking rhetoric in the twenty-first century reverses the flow of traffic, this time portraying white women as forced to *enter*, not *leave*, Britain.

After the 2004 and 2007 EU accessions, East European member states entered into a new relationship with Western Europe. The EU sets the standards for membership and decides which countries can join. Accession depends on eradicating differences in an unequal geopolitical field of power. Membership materializes if East European countries can convince the EU that they are ready to (re)join Europe. To be included, countries must possess Western assets that are defined as a free-market economy, a stable democracy, and the rule of law. Countries should also accept EU legislation and the euro as their currency.[24] Member states can opt out of EU legislation and treaties. Indeed, the UK was the least integrated EU member state, with four opt-outs including the euro, the Charter of Fundamental Rights, Schengen Area, and Area of Freedom, Security and Justice. Yet in a power move that elides the racism, discrimination, and lapses in the rule of law of Western EU states, new EU members need to demonstrate compliance, including a respect for and protection of minorities and human rights.

Identifying imperial logics in the EU project, literary scholar Anca Parvulescu observes how the "civilizing mission has been premised on colonial generosity aimed at helping colonies catch up with the great civilization."[25] The UK likewise speaks in a colonial tongue, employing trafficking rhetoric to accuse other countries of being the sources of sex slavery and uncivilized violence. Trafficking rhetoric revives colonial narratives that say Western nations save women and children from their own kin and countrymen. As scholar of law Elizabeth A. Faulkner notes, trafficking rhetoric "echoes colonial imagery, with individuals framed as victims of their society, from which they require liberation by the morally guided rescuer."[26] The British Empire nurtured an imperial ideology, drenched in dreams of white supremacy, to justify theft and exploitation of lands and peoples. This key point underscores how the colonial claim of giving is always, in fact, a material form of taking that refuses to engage others on equal terms.

Barring the door is nothing new. The British Empire reached across the globe but resisted others entering the *mother country*. Difference, whether construed as racial, cultural, religious, or political, is pointed to as proof that some people cannot assimilate and should be kept out. Others must be desired to be welcomed within. Trafficking rhetoric echoes the white slavery tales that depicted East European Jews as perennial foreigners who sold English women

---

24. Parvulescu, *Traffic in Women's Work*, 3.
25. Parvulescu, *Traffic in Women's Work*, 4.
26. Faulkner, "40.3 Million Slaves."

into prostitution. During Britain's Imperial Century (1815–1914), when it took control of about 10 million square miles and 400 million people, this antisemitic story construed craven behavior as a cultural trait and figured Jewish people as unassimilable.[27] At its core, the empire was an enterprise to manage human bodies, movement, and labor by sending British subjects around the globe to seize people and land and to select who would receive a hospitable or a hostile reception in the home country. The demise of the British Empire, Satnam Virdee and Brendan McGeever argue, "has not led to the overcoming of the English imperial complex, but its retraction into a defensive exclusionary imaginary: we are under siege, it is time to pull up the drawbridge."[28] The EU's supranational scheme to soften borders among member states does not rewrite the West/East and North/South binaries inked in imperial ideology and drawing the world map. The EU manages uneasy flows and stoppages across defeated empires, postcommunist states, and nascent nations to manifest an integrated European geopolitical bloc.

While the EU propounds the principle of the free movement of goods, services, citizens, and capital, that is, the Four Freedoms, the reality is that almost every Western EU state reacted to the inclusion of East Europeans by curbing their rights to move and work within the EU. New EU citizens found themselves excluded by immigration barriers that states erected *in reaction to their inclusion.* Beyond overseeing their entry into the country and various labor sectors, the UK subjected East EU citizens to suspicion, stigma, and surveillance by discursively linking them to crime, while putting a fig leaf over the antitrafficking agenda's violations of human rights and the rule of law.

LEGAL STATES OF EXCEPTION: TRAFFICKING VICTIM / ECONOMIC MIGRANT

The UK government put victims of trafficking into an exceptional category of economic migrant who deserved sympathy and help because they had been subjected to sexual exploitation. In the first decade of the twenty-first century, *sex trafficking* was the primary focus of antitrafficking efforts. The exceptional category divided victims of trafficking from economic migrants defined as willfully breaking laws, in contrast to trafficked women who lacked volition.

The chief executive of a London-based antitrafficking NGO amplified this distinction in an interview:

27. See Parsons, *British Imperial Century*; and Gephardt, *Idea of Europe.*
28. Virdee and McGeever, "Racism, Crisis, Brexit," 1811.

Inevitably, you've got immigration, which traffic is always tarnished with. Anyone who ever does anything, it's "Immigration! Disgusting! They're all coming in." It should be taken out of the equation of trafficking. And then [there's] asylum, "They're coming here to seek asylum. Disgusting!" Asylum should also be taken out of the word "trafficking." They aren't really, there are threads of course, but it is very much a human rights issue.[29]

She suggested that Britons' feelings about immigration could tarnish trafficking victims and took it as a given that immigrants and asylum seekers were objects of disgust. Rhetoric scholars in the US, such as J. David Cisneros and KC Councilor, have explored the framing of people as matters of pollution or disgust in gendered and racialized immigration systems.[30] Regardless of the chief executive's desire to disentangle the threads connecting immigration, asylum, and trafficking, *all* of them are human rights issues. However, if women enter the sex industry willingly, then they are often cast into the category of unwelcome economic migrants. Sympathy and help can only be extended to the women forced into prostitution, not to those who migrate to escape poverty or persecution. Trafficked women must be rhetorically cleansed of the taint of willful migration for work or political refuge. Arguments like this reify, rather than refute, the idea that migrants live off the state and steal jobs from British workers. In this popular strand of xenophobia, migrants are framed as both *benefit scroungers* and *job stealers*. Migrants, asylum seekers, refugees, and trafficking victims all become accused of taking what belongs to British citizens and costing the UK money, in a patently obvious twist on colonial theft.

The discursive incoherence that describes people who migrate as both unwilling to work and willing to work any job coheres into a consensus about migrant threats. For instance, the UK government used the threat of trafficking to criminalize the legal activities of indoor prostitution and EU immigration. In 2004, indoor prostitution was legal (when a person worked indoors and alone), and EU citizens could migrate to the UK (when it had an open-door policy). Trafficking rhetoric pointed to indoor prostitution and EU migration as housing "sex slavery," turning them into targets of law and immigration enforcement as a strategy "to ensure that the UK becomes a hostile environment for traffickers."[31]

---

29. Interview field notes, October 22, 2009. Tellingly, immigration is said to tarnish trafficking, not the other way around, which is quite a twist in logic.

30. See Cisneros, "Contaminated Communities"; and Councilor, "Feeding the Body Politic."

31. Association of Chief Police Officers in Scotland, "Operation Pentameter 2."

Rhetorically tying immigration and prostitution to trafficking bound concerns over labor exploitation to a tiny subset of (female) migrants, thereby ensuring that the people the UK will help stays small and contained. Recipients of state help are reduced while the UK expands the sense of threat by suggesting that any economic migrant could be a trafficker or a trafficking victim. The torque of containment and expansion bolsters state power by making the modest number of people receiving help into an occasion to celebrate British benevolence. Meanwhile, police and immigration officers search the country for the hidden traffic in foreign women. The Home Office portrayed "measures to prevent irregular forms of migration as though they were simultaneously anti-trafficking measures," sociologist Julia O'Connell Davidson explains, and the "authorities charged with a responsibility to contain illegal migration and combat organized crime" were said to be rescuing trafficking victims.[32] In this way, the "recoding of the complex transnational dynamics of labor and migration through the lens of trafficking has legitimized the dramatic expansion of policing and security-based interventions."[33] Decades of tolerance toward indoor prostitution ended in favor of nationwide anti-trafficking raids.[34] Trafficking rhetoric thus rationalizes state violence under the pretext of fighting crime (securing the nation) and protecting vulnerable women (saving sex slaves).

East Europeans were tagged as potential traffickers or victims, but Britons were heralded as a nation with a venerable history of freeing slaves. This narrative whitewashed British history, with its slave trading also rebranded as an aberration made right by abolition. "The (ab)use of the term 'abolition' by anti-prostitution crusaders appropriating Black suffering" exacerbates harms and violence, particularly against Black women, whether they are, or are assumed to be, working in the sex trade.[35] This type of (ab)use goes back a long way. British, West European, and North American feminists in the late nineteenth century mobilized the term *abolition* to declare that the sex trade was analogous to the slave trade, ergo, prostitution was sexual slavery.[36] As sociologist Elizabeth Bernstein incisively observed, liberal feminists in the early twenty-first century shared with their predecessors the idea that states should stamp out sex work. In the renewed movement to abolish prostitution, Bernstein argued, antitrafficking advocates pushed for punitive neoliberal "solutions to contemporary social problems, with trafficking or so-called

32. O'Connell Davidson, "Will the Real Sex Slave," 10.
33. Heynen and van der Meulen, "Anti-Trafficking Saviors," 3.
34. Hill, "How to Stage a Raid"; and Hill, "Demanding Victims."
35. Maynard, "Do Black Sex Workers' Lives Matter?," 282.
36. Bernstein, "Militarized Humanism Meets Carceral Feminism," 46.

'modern-day slavery' representing the antithesis of low-wage work in the pur-
portedly free market."[37] But this stance "obscures the ways in which the actual
history of transatlantic slavery undergirds contemporary global exploitation,"
and it solicits the power to punish, endorsing state violence in the name of
stopping sexual violence against women.[38]

Fabulating a transhistorical British abolitionism, UK trafficking rhetoric
indexes gender, race, and nationality as indicators of criminal violence and
sexual victimization. As a racializing rhetoric, it conceals itself by presenting
human trafficking as a postracial problem. *Modern-day slavery* is modern in
this sense because *anyone* can be trafficked now. Whites can be subjected to
the dehumanization of slavery, and that changes things. As rhetoric scholar
Leslie Harris argues, the portrayal of white women as exceptionally vulnerable
to enslavement depends on imagining the unique innocence and violability of
white femininity.[39] Stories of white women forced into sexual slavery attracts
intense attention to the subject of trafficking, pulling resources toward anti-
prostitution and anti-immigration campaigns while depicting some migrants
as innocent and others as illegal. Appropriating the rhetoric of abolition to
advance its antitrafficking agenda, the UK government racializes East Europeans as peripherally white, as secondary to West European and British whiteness, and as unable to save themselves from criminality and sexual violence.

Antitrafficking rhetoric presents human trafficking as an exogenic problem, to which the UK reacts without ever being implicated in its constitutive
conditions. "Framed as a violation of bodily integrity and problem of criminal behavior," feminist scholar Jennifer Suchland explains, "human trafficking
gained recognition as an aberration of capitalist systems."[40] Weaving carceral
and capitalist systems together as antithetical to trafficking hides "how trafficking is intertwined in the constitutive operations of economic systems."[41]
Instead, the UK is cast as simply a victim of transnational crime and unwanted
EU migration. The victim of trafficking comes to symbolize the UK's subordination to the EU. Accusations about lost sovereignty got louder during the
2016 Brexit referendum, which led to the UK becoming the first country to
exit the EU. That fateful decision responded to ardent calls for the UK to free
itself from EU entanglements by reclaiming its stolen sovereignty.

The conceit was that without the UK's absolute sovereignty to decide who
immigrated, unwelcome people would proliferate, and the face of Britain

---

37. Bernstein, "Militarized Humanism Meets Carceral Feminism," 47.
38. Beutin, "There's a Trafficking Jam on the Underground Railroad," 3.
39. Harris, *Rhetoric of White Slavery*; and Harris, "Rhetorical Mobilities and the City."
40. Suchland, *Economies of Violence*, 1.
41. Suchland, *Economies of Violence*, 1.

would change forever. It followed that the EU posed an existential threat to Great Britain as it tried to become Global Britain. "To speak of a Global Britain is to not only suggest how great Britain can be in the future," Virdee and McGeever write, "but also to invoke warm collective memories of a now lost world where Britain was the global hegemon of the capitalist world economy."[42] Contrary to the image of the EU dominating the UK, Global Britain calls to mind "those glory days of economic, political and cultural superiority, where everything from ships to spoons were marked with a *Made in Britain* stamp."[43]

Boasting the most deregulated labor market in the EU, the UK privileges corporations at the expense of citizen and migrant workers. It erects a legal framework excluding undocumented workers from labor protections like nonpayment of wages, unfair dismissal, and discrimination. Routine and extreme labor exploitation occurs in a workforce made impoverished and insecure by the neoliberal policies that structure the UK's deregulated market. According to Hodkinson and coauthors, the "conflation of modern slavery as primarily a law and border enforcement issue targeting criminal gangs *excludes* consideration of how the state itself acts as a 'third party enslaver' through hostile environment policies."[44] They argue that the UK structures and abets the severe exploitation of migrants in three ways: (1) compulsion to enter precarious work; (2) vulnerabilization through the removal of rights and protections; and (3) entrapment in forced labor.[45] The UK links the transatlantic slave trade with human trafficking, while disavowing the links between its deregulation of the labor market and hostile management of immigration. This bogus historical link is made to sell the antitrafficking agenda as a moral, quintessentially British mission. The UK disempowers migrant workers but invests in law and immigration enforcement that negatively and disproportionately impacts migrant and minority communities. Analyzing the neoliberal mode of governance surfaces another link, one between the antitrafficking agenda and labor exploitation in a neoliberal context of hostile sentiment and eroded rights and protections. Thus, I contextualize and interrogate the UK government's claim of enacting a moral response to *modern-day slavery,* that is, of saving migrants from traffickers who control their movement and exploit their labor.

---

42. Virdee and McGeever, "Racism, Crisis, Brexit," 1805.
43. Virdee and McGeever, "Racism, Crisis, Brexit," 1805.
44. Hodkinson et al., "Fighting or Fuelling Forced Labour?," 70.
45. Hodkinson et al., "Fighting or Fuelling Forced Labour?"

OVERVIEW OF CHAPTERS

Trafficking Rhetoric juxtaposes the UK's proclaimed rescue approach to human trafficking with its increasingly hostile approach to human migration. I argue that these approaches are, in effect, two sides of the same coin. The UK anti-trafficking agenda directs hostility against migrants, and people who are not viewed as British, through trafficking rhetoric that depicts the UK as tackling transnational crime and freeing slaves, who are often figured as white women from East Europe. Transnational trafficking is said to compel law and immigration enforcement to deter, detain, and deport people. Bolstering this effort, the UK government builds antitrafficking infrastructure into state agencies while partnering with NGOs, media, and corporations. To grasp the antitrafficking agenda at the national level entails attending to related discourses and diverse sites of argument, ranging from numerical representations, to law and policy, to awareness campaigns. Therefore, I engage in rhetorical-material analyses of trafficking estimates (chapter 1); the *UK Action Plan to Tackle Human Trafficking* (chapter 2); and the Blue Blindfold awareness campaign (chapter 3) before I turn to Pentameter 2, an antitrafficking police operation of unprecedented scale, and the National Referral Mechanism, which judged claimants appealing for victim of trafficking status (chapter 4).

Chapter 1, "Speculative Figures: The Rhetorical Material of Trafficking Estimates," takes up two reports, commissioned by the Home Office, that estimated women trafficked for sexual exploitation. The UK government used the estimates to support claims about *modern-day slavery* and to initiate policy and police crackdowns on both prostitution and immigration. The dominant narrative about trafficking interpellated white East European women as sympathetic victims of a shocking crime, and prostitution was said to hide sexual slavery in the UK. This material rhetoric helped to make possible a growing hostility toward prostitution and immigration. Crucial to this narrative, trafficking estimates appeared as objective measures numerically representing victims. The UK government commissioned the estimates, which were made by researchers, reported by the media, and repeated as if they referred to real trafficking victims. But the trafficking estimates relied on proxy groups, including women engaged in prostitution or migrating for marriage. The process of creating estimates made no contact with the people it claimed to count. In the chapter, I analyze the creation and circulation of trafficking estimates to account for how these speculative figures materialized state action against targeted populations. The rhetoric of estimation is vital material because it grounds a neoliberal, seemingly neutral rationale for the UK antitrafficking agenda.

Chapter 2, "Anti-Blackness by Analogy: Human Trafficking and the Rhetoric of Modern-Day Slavery," analyzes the *UK Action Plan to Tackle Human Trafficking*. By closely reading the *Action Plan*'s textual and visual frames, I critique the analogies that tether the transatlantic slave trade to human trafficking, thereby fabricating a conceptual chain between abolition and the UK antitrafficking plan. I recover the historical facts that the *Action Plan* suppresses through its self-serving abolition story, which centers and celebrates Britain's triumph over the slave trade. That hagiography portrays Britain as committed to stopping slavery (again) via a strategic retelling of historical abolition that serves to promote the UK antitrafficking agenda. I weigh in on this story by interrogating the *Action Plan*'s analogical links and drawing on archival work on the British Empire, slave trade, and moral panic over so-called white slavery, that is, the forced migration and prostitution of English women and girls. By providing a fuller history, I surface the ties that bind Britain's past and present, which brings up how the UK deploys extraterritorial governance to pressure other sovereign states to align with British interests and antitrafficking initiatives.

Chapter 3, "Glaring Whiteness: Trafficking Visual Rhetoric and Tropes of Blindness," focuses on an antitrafficking awareness campaign called Blue Blindfold, coordinated by the UK Human Trafficking Centre (UKHTC). The chapter analyzes the UK government's appeals not only to rationality through estimates but also to sentimentality through antitrafficking imagery. Blue Blindfold exhibited representations of Britons in blindfolds, to symbolize their inability to see the trafficking happening right under their noses. Without visualizing traffickers or victims, campaign posters instead depict Britons as "blind" to say that seeing victims requires watchful citizens. I identify Blue Blindfold's visual enthymeme to parse its hidden premise and blatant but unstated xenophobia and racism. The chapter tracks the blindfold trope's reappearance amid the Brexit debates to grasp how the enthymeme shifts, yet in significant ways stays the same, when the discursive and material contexts change. I argue that the Blue Blindfold awareness campaign incites the criminal profiling of migrants and minority citizens whose appearance is not seen as British, meaning, in material terms, as white. Performing a rhetorical-material analysis of Blue Blindfold, and blindfold Brexit, reveals that they each express and encourage anxieties over the UK's geopolitical position while prescribing different cures for British "blindness."

Chapter 4, "'A Really Hostile Environment for Illegal Migrants': State Violence, Misery, and Immobility" traces the Conservative government's Hostile Environment Policy in 2012 back to the Labour Party's turn from an open-door immigration policy after the EU expansion in 2004. The chapter analyzes the UK's largest antitrafficking operation, code-named Pentameter 2, which was celebrated as a success until a journalist exposed that it had failed to find anyone forced into prostitution. This shocking outcome suggested that even when antitrafficking raids do not locate victims, they succeed in promoting more policing, never less. The National Referral Mechanism (NRM), set up to process people appealing for victim of trafficking status, also contradicted the dominant trafficking narrative. The NRM outcome statistics recognized UK nationals as victims of trafficking more often than any other nationality. That statistical skew highlights the hardship that migrants faced in obtaining recognition as victims, despite the state story that trafficking was an exogenous crime. The UK government continued to claim it was saving migrant women from criminal gangs and sexual slavery. Turning to Pentameter 2 and the NRM, I end my longitudinal study, which began with the creation of trafficking estimates and concludes by investigating the human costs of the UK's antitrafficking infrastructure and really hostile environment.

Lastly, the conclusion offers reflections on the antitrafficking agenda's connection to the 2018 Windrush scandal, which put the hostile treatment of migrants and minority citizens at the forefront of a national conversation about race, history, labor, and citizenship. Due to the Hostile Environment Policy, citizens who had migrated decades earlier from Commonwealth Caribbean countries had been wrongfully detained, denied their legal rights, and, in some cases, deported.[46] Reading this scandal through the lessons of the antitrafficking agenda that preceded it, I consider the methodological pathways that *Trafficking Rhetoric* opens up for future work using rhetorical-material analysis to grasp who is rendered immaterial and why.

Before turning to the chapters, let me return briefly to my opening discussion of events in Bristol to consider what happened after Black Lives Matter protesters felled Colston's statue and what these events might tell us about the UK's political landscape.

---

46. After World War II, the British government invited Commonwealth citizens from the West Indies to migrate and to help rebuild Britain. They became known as the *Windrush generation* because one of the first groups crossed the Atlantic Ocean on the *Empire Windrush*. The vessel had a complex history. Taken from the Nazis by the British in the war, it had been a cruise ship, troop carrier, and prison ship used to deport Jews before the British repurposed it as a passenger liner for Commonwealth citizens who paid for their journey to a new life in the UK.

INSURGENCE: THE URGENT MATTER OF SLAVERY

After Colston had been brought down, a Black woman named Jen Reid climbed up on the plinth and raised her fist in the air. She later said of her action,

> Knowing what Colston represented, I felt compelled to take a stand and raise my fist in empowerment for the slaves who died at his hands. It was like an electrical surge of power was running through me as I took the plinth in memory of George Floyd, and for every black person killed by police for being black, and those who face injustice daily based on the colour of their skin.[47]

An iconic photograph of this moment showed Reid standing as a monument to Black pride and power. Many people found the sight moving and talked about it as a sign of change in the UK's reckoning with the past and recognition of Black Britons in the present.

On July 15, a sculpture of Reid, made from black resin and titled *A Surge of Power (Jen Reid) 2020*, was placed on the plinth where Colston once stood (see figure 2). Gazing up at her sculpture, Reid remarked, "That's pretty fucking ballsy, that it is."[48] And it was. Marc Quinn, an artist who made the artwork with Reid, did not have Bristol City Council's permission to install it publicly. Discussing the replica of Reid and the urgent need to display it, Quinn said, "Racism is a huge problem, a virus that needs to be addressed." Then he added, "I hope this sculpture will continue that dialogue, keep it in the forefront of people's minds, be an energy conductor."[49]

The Colston statue stood for more than a century in Bristol, but the city council removed the sculpture of Reid in twenty-four hours.[50] In response to the alacrity, she concluded, "Whether it's there for a day or a week or a month, it's been there."[51] The monumental work representing a Black woman who stood against racist state violence was testament to the insurgent possibilities of cultural change and collective resistance. The city council retrieved Colston's statue from the river and put it on display in a local museum, still marred by paint and on its side due to damage at its base. The state pointed

---

47. Emelife, "'Hope Flows through This Statue.'"

48. Bland, "Edward Colston Statue Replaced."

49. Emelife, "'Hope Flows through This Statue.'"

50. Bristol's lord mayor, Marvin Rees, has the distinction of being the first directly elected Black mayor in Europe. His British background is rather more typical: his mother was white and born in Britain, and his father migrated from Jamaica in the 1960s as part of the Windrush generation.

51. Bland, "Black Lives Matter Sculpture."

FIGURE 2. Jen Reid statue in Bristol, UK.
Used with permission from Alamy.

to the supposed misdeeds of the BLM protesters to distract from its veneration of a slave trader and to punish people who dared to take matters into
their own hands. Four protesters who helped topple the Colston statue were
picked out and charged with criminal damage. The Colston Four trial at Bristol Crown Court exposed the state's anxious reaction to what *The Guardian*
called "one of the most significant and symbolic acts of public dissent in Britain this century."[52] In 2022 a jury acquitted the Colston Four, thus affirming
that their actions were justified due to the moral offense caused by the statue
of Colston.

The torque of state violence and state veneration is evidenced in the rapid
removal of Reid's sculpture, the subjection of BLM protesters to a criminal
trial, and the Windrush scandal, which developed from the UK's hostile

52. Gayle, "How Bristol Came Out."

approach to migrant and minority communities. Political sociologist William Walters caricatures the punitive logic animating the hostile approach: "If we can just identify the genuine refugee, or the high-skilled migrant, this will allow us to deal with the others, the 'bogus,' with greater confidence from the public and thus with more firmness."[53] Trafficking rhetoric depends on a stigmatic story about a surge in crime and unwanted migration to engage in the coercive categorizing, sorting, and (mis)identifying of people under the guise of stopping *modern-day slavery*. That this state violence severely impacted nonwhite migrants and minority citizens stresses how antitrafficking agendas are made out of the matter of race, gender, labor, and unequal levels of citizenship. The sense of urgency in the UK over *sex trafficking* was stunning given its thin evidentiary base and, even more so, when compared to the sluggish state responses to anti-Black violence despite decades of overwhelming evidence of structural racism and discrimination. Conjuring the horror of *white unfreedom*, the UK government disavowed the logics and legacies of transatlantic slavery and white supremacy riddling the world to this day.

53. Walters, "Secure Borders, Safe Haven, Domopolitics," 249.

CHAPTER 1

Speculative Figures

The Rhetorical Material of Trafficking Estimates

As the state department responsible for national security and immigration, the United Kingdom's Home Office commissioned two reports to estimate how many women had been trafficked to the UK for sexual exploitation in 1998 and 2003, respectively.[1] Both of the reports explained that the estimates were speculative since it was impossible to know the real number of trafficked women. But the speculative nature of these numbers did not stop their circulation as material evidence of *sex trafficking*. The UK government relied on the figures while saying little about how they came to be. The dominant narrative of foreign women forcibly transported into prostitution determined how human trafficking was quantified. Trafficking rhetoric's primary focus on cis women at this time excluded queer, transgender, and nonbinary people, as well as cis men, from recognition as potential victims of trafficking within prostitution and other industries.

At an academic conference where I delivered a paper analyzing the UK's first trafficking estimates, an audience member agreed the numbers sounded implausible, and he wanted to know the real number of trafficked women. For him, the problem was about accurate calculation and appropriate state action, to decide whether the UK was over- or underreacting to *sex trafficking*. He

---

1. The reports are titled, respectively, *Stopping Traffic: Exploring the Extent of, and Responses to, Trafficking in Women for Sexual Exploitation in the UK* and *The Impact of Organised Crime in the UK: Revenues and Economic and Social Costs.*

then made a claim I had heard many times; he insisted that if estimates of trafficked women were wrong, then the right number must be larger. The basis for this claim went unstated, but his reasoning perfectly captured how quantification has been applied to trafficking. Critiques of the estimates generate calls for more and better numbers, with estimates assumed to be undercounts. The drive to quantify trafficking rests on the assumption that if the current estimate is wrong, the right number is sure to come! I replied to my interlocutor that it is the impossibility of finding the real figure that enables trafficking estimates to proliferate and persuade. These nonstop numbers, however, ultimately depend on locating actual victims of trafficking.[2]

I argued that estimates were the problem, not due to their inaccuracy but because of their rhetorical efficacy in making trafficking real to publics and authorizing repressive state agendas. Estimates informed how governments, police, media, NGOs, and publics understood trafficking (often as hidden, growing, and spreading). In this chapter, I show that the UK trafficking figures were seen as more real and reliable than the women they claimed to count. It is therefore crucial to grasp the matter of trafficking numbers and their rhetorical power in galvanizing state action. In what follows, I investigate the UK estimates that made trafficking come to life in a seemingly empirical way.

Trafficking estimates rely on epistemic authority and appear to be objective measures and reflections of reality. Yet dubious data and unsound methods often serve as the pseudoscientific grounds that support claims about the nature and extent of human trafficking. Criticizing Brazil's estimate of trafficking, for example, Thaddeus Gregory Blanchette and Ana Paula da Silva argue, "methodologically sound scientific research is not as useful as the promulgation of spectacular claims based on spurious data."[3] To show how trafficking came to be a state problem, I analyze the neoliberal discourses of evidence-based research and data-driven policy used by politicians, police, researchers, journalists, policymakers, and antitrafficking advocates. I handle trafficking estimates as rhetorical material to grasp how they mediate dual desires for rational policy and for passionate moral crusades to rescue trafficked women.

First, rather than being recognized as highly speculative figures, trafficking estimates are presented and perceived as if they represent real victims, setting up a false equivalence between numbers and human referents. Second, trafficking estimates translate complex social phenomena involving migration,

---

2. See O'Connell Davidson, "Will the Real Sex Slave?"

3. Blanchette and da Silva, "On Bullshit," 122. Other strong critiques of trafficking definitions, data, and estimates include Chapkis, "Trafficking, Migration, and the Law"; Chuang, "Rescuing Trafficking from Ideological Capture"; Yea, "The Politics of Evidence"; and Musto, "What's in a Name?"

exploitation, and violence into a manageable problem, with not only a name but a specific number. Writing about the seductions of quantification, anthropologist Sally Engle Merry contends that estimates "presume that [complex social issues] are countable phenomena."[4] Third, trafficking estimates come alive when they move from original reports into new discursive contexts. Former director of UNESCO's Bangkok program on trafficking and HIV/AIDS, David Feingold, warns of the persuasive power, or life force, of speculative figures:

> Numbers take on a life of their own, gaining acceptance through repetition, often with little inquiry into their derivations. Journalists—bowing to the pressures of editors—demand numbers, any numbers. Organizations feel compelled to supply them, lending false precision and spurious authority to many reports.[5]

The rhetorical life of trafficking estimates manifests as they travel through texts, gaining traction and validity as empirical claims. Estimates help antitrafficking agendas to go live, circulating as statistical counterparts to sensationalistic stories about sex slavery. Official numbers speak to the existence of trafficking victims which, in turn, justifies antitrafficking law, policy, and policing. "To measure something—or at least claim to do so," political scientists Peter Andreas and Kelly M. Greenhill note, "is to announce its existence and signal its importance and policy relevance."[6] Trafficking estimates announced the arrival of foreign women forced into prostitution in the UK. According to communication scholar Lyndsey P. Beutin,

> Antitrafficking advocacy has used the rhetoric and aesthetics of a scientific approach to slavery to justify modern slavery's existence since 1999. The hallmarks of this approach include: quantification (of people, of degrees of exploitation, of NGO project outputs), data visualizations, devising and promoting replicable models, and performing neutrality.[7]

The estimates transmogrify trafficking into a measurable problem that states can solve. But, as Blastland and Dilnot express it in *The Numbers Game*, bad estimates result in "bad policy, bad government, gobbledygook news, . . . lost

---

4. Merry, *Seductions of Quantification*, 19. See also Fedina, "Use and Misuse of Research."
5. Feingold, "Trafficking in Numbers," 52.
6. Andreas and Greenhill, *Sex, Drugs, and Body Counts*, 1.
7. Beutin, *Trafficking in Antiblackness*, 135.

chances and screwed-up lives."[8] According to Andreas and Greenhill, numbers are "born bad" when based on inaccurate data, incorrect methodologies, or unclear measurements.[9] Numbers "go bad" when they are misinterpreted or distorted. In this chapter, I seek to show that the UK's initial estimates of trafficking were born bad and got worse when they moved from original reports into new discursive contexts. As the trafficking estimates traveled, they were rounded up, stripped of disclaimers, and used loosely to represent different groups (sometimes trafficked women, sometimes trafficked women and men, sometimes migrant women involved in prostitution, and sometimes a percentage of all prostitutes in the UK). I track the estimates' creation and circulation to plot out how these speculative figures supported a state antitrafficking agenda and spoke for the group(s) they were calculated to count.

In subsequent pages, I follow the data and methods in the aforementioned reports as well as an NGO report to pinpoint the anti-prostitution ideology propelling the sex trafficking figures. To perform a rhetorical-material analysis of trafficking estimates, I must account for the ideological values and animating assumptions congealed in numeric rhetoric, together with what these numbers help to make happen. Counting facilitates controlling.

FOUNDATIONAL FIGURE:
THE FIRST UK TRAFFICKING ESTIMATE

When attempts to measure trafficking commenced, no laws in the United Kingdom expressly prohibited that phenomenon. The Sexual Offences Act 1956 did outlaw prostitution and sexual exploitation but lacked offenses that specifically outlined trafficking. Offenses that could apply to trafficking cases originated from the nineteenth-century crusade against the forced transport and prostitution of English women, known as "white slavery." In the 1990s, however, growing international alarm about human trafficking highlighted the UK's lack of relevant legislation. Its legal landscape was ill-equipped to tackle human trafficking. It also needed to decriminalize old offenses like buggery and combat new abuses like cyberstalking. During the legislative overhaul of the Sexual Offences Act 1956, the Home Office wanted an estimate of the number of women trafficked for sexual exploitation. In addition to providing the estimate, this commissioned report declared that "new law should be

---

8. Blastland and Dilnot, *Numbers Game,* xii.

9. Andreas and Greenhill draw on Joel Best's claim that some statistics are born bad (2). See Best, *Damned Lies and Statistics.*

drafted to aid detection and prosecution of trafficking, with sentences that are likely to have a significant deterrent effect."[10] The process of estimation fused with the promise of criminalization from the outset.

The sixty-two-page report was written by Liz Kelly and Linda Regan. At the time, Kelly served as director of the Child and Woman Abuse Studies Unit, then located at the University of North London, where Regan worked as a research officer. Titled *Stopping Traffic: Exploring the Extent of, and Responses to, Trafficking in Women for Sexual Exploitation in the UK,* Kelly and Regan introduce it as "an exploratory study, commissioned by the Home Office Policing and Reducing Crime Unit (PRCU), focusing on the nature and extent of trafficking in women for the purposes of sexual exploitation in the UK."[11] As the title indicates, the goal was also to influence policy. Hence, Kelly and Regan make the crucial claim that the study moves "'beyond anecdote' to account for the number of cases known to police in 1998, and other data which suggest the wider scale of the problem."[12] But in a section titled "Of Needles and Haystacks: Methodology," they compare estimating trafficking "to looking for needles in haystacks," which underscores the difficulty of translating complex social phenomena into a number.[13] Kelly and Regan maintain it is possible, however, if they create an estimate range rather than trying to find a precise figure. In their words,

> one possible method of sidestepping the numbers debate is to present estimates within a range from the minimum (for which there is an accurate base) to a theoretical, and speculative, maximum (which relies on less substantiated material).[14]

Kelly and Regan take what they say were confirmed cases of trafficking, add in an assortment of other material, and extrapolate from there to create the maximum figure for their range. But their sources and method suggest that anti-prostitution abolitionism underpins the math.

---

10. Kelly and Regan, *Stopping Traffic,* 11.

11. Kelly and Regan, *Stopping Traffic,* 6. Within the Home Office's Research Development and Statistics Directorate, the PRCU commissioned and conducted research on policing and crime. Its Police Research Series focused on crime prevention and detection as well as police management and organization.

12. Kelly and Regan, *Stopping Traffic,* 16.

13. Kelly and Regan, *Stopping Traffic,* 6.

14. Kelly and Regan, *Stopping Traffic,* 16.

Assume the Unknown:
The Method for Making Trafficking Estimates

To estimate trafficking in the UK, Kelly and Regan sent a questionnaire survey to the forty-three police forces in England and Wales. They received responses from thirty-six forces (a 78 percent response rate), signaling a high level of cooperation with this study for the Home Office. Kelly and Regan explain that the responses indicated that "the minimum number of women trafficked in the UK and known to the police in 1998 is 71."[15] This police figure forms the "accurate base" on which Kelly and Regan construct an estimate range. They add nine more sources to arrive at a "theoretical, and speculative, maximum" number.[16] Below, I detail their source inventory to show what Kelly and Regan counted as persuasive material evidence of trafficked women.

1. Referring to the police data, Kelly and Regan state, "The research revealed at least six possible additional cases that might have lead [*sic*] to knowledge about the number of trafficked women."[17] As such, they endeavor to build on the "accurate base" of seventy-one police cases.

2. Two unnamed sources gave "information on the UK being used as a transit country," particularly of West African girls and women.[18] According to Kelly and Regan, the "traffic of West African girls, and especially Nigerians, into the Italian sex industry has been known for some years," resulting in immigration controls targeting Africans on direct flights to Italy. They state that there are fewer immigration controls on UK flights to Italy, "since significant numbers of Black British young people travel to Italy for holidays and school trips."[19] The implication is that the risk of racially profiling Black British passengers leads to fewer controls on travel. Kelly and Regan add, "The Immigration Service have information from all London airports and know of about 50–60 West African girls and young women who have been moved through the UK."[20] But no explanation is given about how the Immigration Service knew the West African girls and women were trafficked or whether the UK assisted them based on that knowledge.

3. Kelly and Regan note that the Clubs and Vice Unit of the London Metropolitan Police "check[s] flats known to be used for prostitution in the Soho

---

15. Kelly and Regan, *Stopping Traffic*, 18.
16. Kelly and Regan, *Stopping Traffic*, 16.
17. Kelly and Regan, *Stopping Traffic*, 19.
18. Kelly and Regan, *Stopping Traffic*, 19.
19. Kelly and Regan, *Stopping Traffic*, 19.
20. Kelly and Regan, *Stopping Traffic*, 19.

area every six weeks to ensure there are no minors working there."[21] During the spring of 1999, this unit checked fifty flats, and "the majority of women working there were found to be migrants."[22] On that basis, Kelly and Regan state, "Whilst it cannot be presumed that all of these women had been trafficked, it is considered likely that a proportion of them have been."[23] The comment exemplifies the conflation of *foreign* women with *forced* prostitution, counting them as trafficked women without giving evidence for drawing that conclusion. As will become clear throughout this chapter, the use of conflation is a common rhetorical device in trafficking discourse.

4. Kelly and Regan likewise refer to a Home Office seminar in 1999 where "workers in health projects *were reported to estimate* that 50% of London sex industry workers are migrant women, and that 5% have been trafficked."[24] They do not say who reported these estimates, who the health workers were, or which health projects had this information. Reference to the "London sex industry" differs from *Stopping Traffic*'s focus on "off-street prostitution." Put another way, the source offers estimates for a larger labor sector than Kelly and Regan's other sources since it refers to the entire sex industry in London, although what that includes is not explained either. No evidence beyond secondhand statements supports such notably neat percentages.

5. Next, Kelly and Regan add the Home Office's Organised Crime Notification Scheme, which "lists eight groups that are known to be involved both in the traffic of human beings and prostitution."[25] The broader category of "traffic of human beings" includes more industries than prostitution. Kelly and Regan clarify that only two of these eight groups "limit their activities to trafficking in women for prostitution."[26] They do not name the other activities involved, but they use the source to claim, "At least two of these groups are potentially additional to the confirmed cases [of trafficking] discussed previously, since either their nationality or area of operation did not correlate with information provided by [police] forces in the current resrearch [*sic*]."[27]

6. In addition to state sources they list including the police, the Immigration Service, the Clubs and Vice Unit, a Home Office seminar, and the Organised Crime Notification Scheme, Kelly and Regan cite one news story. Headlined "Kosovo Sex Slaves Held in Soho Flats," this *Times* story from 1999

21. Kelly and Regan, *Stopping Traffic*, 19.
22. Kelly and Regan, *Stopping Traffic*, 19.
23. Kelly and Regan, *Stopping Traffic*, 20.
24. Kelly and Regan, *Stopping Traffic*, 20. My emphasis.
25. Kelly and Regan, *Stopping Traffic*, 20.
26. Kelly and Regan, *Stopping Traffic*, 20.
27. Kelly and Regan, *Stopping Traffic*, 20.

exemplifies the trope of the Eastern sex slave circulating at the time. Kelly and Regan believe that this news story "points to the presence of trafficked women in areas of the UK where the police forces have not identified it as a problem."[28] Their use of this source brings us back to the reliance of Brazil's trafficking estimate on newspaper stories, which, Blanchette and da Silva argue, "are not a reliable source of data for sensationalistic topics like trafficking of people."[29] Through a conflation of *country of origin* with *victim of trafficking*, Kelly and Regan assume the unknown and turn a dubious news story into an official data source.

7. Kelly and Regan similarly turn to the internet as a source of data by looking for online ads of sexual services. They report finding ads "confirming that there is off-street prostitution in a number of [police] force areas where the survey responses suggested no such activity."[30] Once again, they give a calculated equivocation: "It cannot be assumed that the women referred to in these adverts had been trafficked, but neither can it be assumed that they had not."[31] Yet, as with the presence of migrant prostitutes in London (data source 3), they see *representations* of women in online ads as trafficking indicators, and they factor these ads into the estimate, although online ads should not be taken as empirical descriptions of reality.

8. Still focused on the internet, Kelly and Regan observe, "Marriage agencies are another area in which trafficking in women is suspected, [and] these have increasingly shifted advertising 'online.'"[32] In their view, the websites of marriage agencies represent women "as commodities to be purchased," and thus the sites become material sources as potential avenues for trafficking.[33]

9. Finally, Kelly and Regan remark that "immigration statistics on the origins of women entering the UK as overseas wives or fiancées offers additional food for thought."[34] Most women come from the Indian subcontinent and United States. Those origin countries, according to Kelly and Regan, indicate "likely sources of chosen marriage partners" (i.e., nontrafficked women). It is revealing to the researchers, however, "the numbers of women entering from countries where trafficking is a known concern, and which are favoured source countries for mail order bride agencies."[35] In *Trafficking Women's*

28. Kelly and Regan, *Stopping Traffic*, 20.
29. Blanchette and da Silva, "On Bullshit," 112.
30. Kelly and Regan, *Stopping Traffic*, 20.
31. Kelly and Regan, *Stopping Traffic*, 20.
32. Kelly and Regan, *Stopping Traffic*, 20.
33. Kelly and Regan, *Stopping Traffic*, 21.
34. Kelly and Regan, *Stopping Traffic*, 21.
35. Kelly and Regan, *Stopping Traffic*, 21.

Human Rights, gender studies scholar Julietta Hua contends that the idea of love-based, and hence legitimate, marriage "works as a regulatory norm to police national borders and the boundaries of citizenship."[36] Their questionable source, and the eight that preceded it, congeals ideological values within numeric rhetoric. Normative ideas about "chosen" marriage and immigration, for instance, determined what was counted as significant material for estimating trafficked women.

The final four sources demonstrate that Kelly and Regan assumed women were trafficked through off-street prostitution, online ads for sexual services, marriage agencies, and migration for marriage. A hypothesis that trafficking for sexual exploitation was organized via these routes needed to be ascertained, not assumed. Kelly and Regan, however, turn their hypothesis into fact to build on the police figure and produce a bigger number. Any links between immigration to the UK and trafficking for sexual exploitation were precisely the unknowns that needed to be established to produce an estimate of trafficked women. In the following extract taken from *Stopping Traffic,* I italicize key verbs to stress the series of animating assumptions configuring this estimate range. Explaining the method, Kelly and Regan write,

> *Assuming* that a higher proportion than the 25% of migrant women in the sex industry have been trafficked . . . ; *taking* the journalistic estimates of "hundreds" of women from Albania and Kosovo as accurate . . . ; *postulating* greater involvement of trafficked women outside London . . . *including* women who enter as mail order brides . . . and *including* a significant amount of internal trafficking . . . provides us with a figure of twenty times larger than confirmed cases.[37]

The verbs *assuming, taking,* and *postulating* evince that the numbers are not evidence-based but the sum of speculations. Kelly and Regan are candid about the conjecture, however that candor is belied by the confident (and incredible) claim that *Stopping Traffic* moves from anecdote toward evidence. Based on the source materials, Kelly and Regan conclude, "it can be estimated that the true scale of trafficking may be between two and twenty times that which has been confirmed."[38] Therefore, they estimate that between 142 and 1,420 women were trafficked in 1998 in the UK. While the range is wide, the numbers themselves are precise enough to lend them an appearance of accuracy. The range presented, for example, is not between 140 and 1,400. Rounder numbers

36. Hua, *Trafficking Women's Human Rights,* 37.
37. Kelly and Regan, *Stopping Traffic,* 22. My emphasis.
38. Kelly and Regan, *Stopping Traffic,* 21.

would highlight that the estimate range is not only really wide but also vague. Precise-sounding numbers make trafficking estimates feel concrete.[39] And numbers function as pathetic appeals by eliciting public feelings on a sensitive policy issue, thereby satisfying the dual desires for rational policymaking and passionate crusades to save trafficked women. After all, an estimated range of between 142 and 1,420 women sounds like a reasonable number for the state to save from sex slavery!

Significantly, Kelly and Regan's earlier admission that they relied on "less substantiated material" to create a "speculative maximum" morphs here to a bold claim about the "true scale of trafficking." Presenting estimates as non-rhetorical facts obscures their rhetorical invention in the service of a political argument. Further, Kelly and Regan's avowal that their base number "has been confirmed" implies that they verified the data sent by police forces, as opposed to simply accepting the material and calling it an "accurate base." Speculative figures representing women confirmed the ideological connection between prostitution and trafficking as empirical truth.

As the next section details, *Stopping Traffic* starts with police forces as its primary source and ends by calling for more policing as a solution to trafficking. Obviously, this state-sponsored calculation is not simply an arithmetic exercise. *Stopping Traffic* succeeds in its suasive ambition to shape state and public responses, although the report resides in the sphere of speculation rather than the realm of empiricism. *Stopping Traffic* effectively sets in motion a range of symbolic and material effects by galvanizing policy and policing to tackle trafficking at the site of prostitution.

Seeing Is Policing: Trafficked Women Everywhere

A way to make sense of Kelly and Regan's methodological choices is to foreground the ideology guiding the estimate's creation and circulation. The first page of *Stopping Traffic* states:

> Whilst much international policy documentation attempts to draw boundaries between trafficking in women and prostitution, it may be suggested that such clear demarcations are problematic. Trafficking in women for the

---

39. Farrell, "Sizing Things Up." Reading Aristotle, Farrell notes about *megethos* (magnitude) that there has to be a level of concreteness that is not too big or too small. Audiences must be able to "see" the scale of a thing to comprehend it and, thus, to be persuaded about it. My thanks to Lisa Flores for raising this point.

purposes of sexual exploitation relies upon, and sustains, prostitution and women's inequality.[40]

This statement stakes out an abolitionist position, viewing prostitution as the subordination of all women. A conceptual matryoshka doll, the position presents human trafficking as hidden within prostitution, which is housed by and born from women's inequality. Notably, class inequality and restrictive immigration policies are not centered as causes of trafficking. Anti-prostitution abolitionists can thus argue that police must target prostitution to attain the political end-goal of eradicating women's inequality. The logic of anti-prostitution abolitionism underpins *Stopping Traffic*'s methodology and recommendation to expand and intensify policing. The section titled "Beyond Anecdotes: Estimating the Trafficking of Women in the UK" opens with an epigraph quoting a police officer who declares, "Wherever there is organised off-street prostitution, our view now is that you will find trafficked women there."[41] Starting from a police point of view validates the assumption that off-street prostitution means the presence of trafficked women. Kelly and Regan aver that their police force survey "found that where there is a reactive, nuisance based, response to prostitution[,] it is less likely that trafficked women will be detected."[42] Consequently, a new ideology—another way of seeing prostitution—is required to detect trafficking and see women in prostitution as victims, not as public nuisances.

Another section is titled "What the Eye Does Not See: Law Enforcement Responses to Trafficking," and it pushes policing toward a proactive framework. In Kelly and Regan's words,

> The pro-active framework begins with the presumption that law enforcement cannot expect trafficking victims either to approach police for protection, or to be able to give evidence. Investigations therefore need to be intelligence led, and use whatever other legal means are available to build a sufficient case to prosecute exploiters at the UK end. If a case involves a willing witness[,] this is seen as "icing on the cake."[43]

Along with prioritizing prosecution, this excerpt expresses both trust in police and anxiety about prostitution going unpoliced. While the proactive approach seems to focus on trafficking victims, it essentially pushes them

---

40. Kelly and Regan, *Stopping Traffic*, 1.
41. Kelly and Regan, *Stopping Traffic*, 16.
42. Kelly and Regan, *Stopping Traffic*, 26.
43. Kelly and Regan, *Stopping Traffic*, 32.

aside to empower police and prosecutors in their pursuit of criminal convictions. Describing "a willing witness" as "icing on the cake," this emphasis on prosecution overrides a woman's will in a way akin to favoring criminalization over the safety and wishes of victims of sexual and intimate partner violence. Privileging carceral responses is conflated with helping helpless victims and ignores how this approach can inflict serious harms on women.

Nevertheless, proceeding with criminal prosecution without victims' willing participation is framed as saving women from the ordeal of a trial and from testifying against traffickers. This framing ignores the fact that victims of trafficking may strongly oppose prosecution and that the UK initially demanded that victims assist police and the prosecution to receive support services. Criticism of this quid pro quo arrangement set up by the state ended the requirement that victims assist law enforcement to obtain support and protection. This coercive practice weakened the UK government's claims about constructing a victim-centered antitrafficking agenda.

Failing to address the risks and potentially harmful effects of proactive policing and using "whatever other legal means are available," Kelly and Regan lament, "Where there is little or no monitoring, activities remain 'unseen,' and therefore unpoliced."[44] They thus argue that off-street prostitution should be seen through an abolitionist lens, which assumes trafficking when migrant women engage in prostitution. It inverts the idea that something must be seen to be believed (i.e., seeing is believing) by instructing police officers to believe trafficking is present even if they do not see it. Trafficking rhetoric interpellates women involved in off-street prostitution as signifiers of *sex trafficking*. Ultimately, Kelly and Regan say that the "most significant barrier [to effective responses to trafficking] appears to be the limited awareness of off-street prostitution throughout police forces."[45] To stop the traffic, then, the solution becomes that prostitution must be policed, which sidesteps that the policing of prostitution materializes as gendered, classed, and racialized profiling and criminal punishment.[46]

Anti-prostitution abolitionism touts policing as an effective response to gender violence, notwithstanding its dismal record responding to sexual and intimate partner violence. Instead, it is assumed that if police start to see prostitutes as victims, then policing will protect, not punish. Kelly and

---

44. Kelly and Regan, *Stopping Traffic*, 28.

45. Kelly and Regan, *Stopping Traffic*, 28.

46. There is copious scholarly literature on policing prostitution in Britain and the British Empire. Exemplars include Laite, *Common Prostitutes and Ordinary Citizens*; Levine, *Prostitution, Race, and Politics*; Phoenix, *Making Sense of Prostitution*; and Walkowitz, *Prostitution and Victorian Society*.

Regan anticipated the Sexual Offences Act 2003, which, a few years after their report, overhauled what the UK defined as sex crimes and how it criminalized offenses. For instance, to erase sexist legal language like the antiquated term "common prostitute," and to fix the one-sided criminalization targeting prostitutes but not clients, the 2003 Act instituted what I term elsewhere a "sympathetic shift" toward women in prostitution.[47] Crucially, this shift starts with mandatory rehabilitative measures to reform prostitutes but (re)turns to criminal penalties if women refuse to exit sex work. Sympathy comes with strings attached, thereby extending the carceral reach of police and state agencies into women's lives.

Beyond supplying estimates to the state, *Stopping Traffic* endorsed the proactive policing of prostitution to discover the trafficked women that it mathematically projected into existence, giving what appears to be an empirical rationale for patrolling prostitutes. For centuries, British law has pursued and punished women working in prostitution; the Sexual Offences Act 2003 was supposed to redress that unjust legal burden. The antitrafficking agenda rebranded the policing of prostitution as an effective and desirable way to protect women from gender violence. However, this argument, seemingly premised on sympathy for women, obscures how policing has been and remains a demonstrable form of gender violence against prostitutes.[48] As *Stopping Traffic* would have it, the frightening alternative to proactive policing is that prostitution will "remain 'unseen,' and therefore unpoliced."

Left unaddressed is whether prostitutes want the police to watch them. Kelly and Regan note that "any recommendation to increase the policing of prostitution will be met with hostility from many women in the sex industry and many of the organizations which support them."[49] The point might have given the researchers food for thought, but the report does not include women's perspectives, or anyone else's, from any sector of sex work. This is a serious limitation given the impact of policing on people's lives and livelihoods and the report's call for proactive policing. It eschews the "nothing about us without us" methodological approach for studying vulnerable groups. As an ethical principle, this methodology incorporates the people who are being studied and who will be affected by the research. Prostitutes are knowledgeable about their industry, but they are rarely seen as experts in their own experience, labor, and workplace. Researchers rely on state and outside sources for

---

47. Hill, "Demanding Victims," 79.

48. My point that policing is a form of gender violence against prostitutes means that, although it is not legible in trafficking rhetoric, policing prostitution targets and harms not only cis women but also queer, transgender, and nonbinary people.

49. Kelly and Regan, *Stopping Traffic,* 37.

information about prostitution and trafficking. Yet *Stopping Traffic* relies rhetorically on the figure of the prostitute; she appears as a mathematical value, a proxy, to prop up its policy argument.[50] Prostitutes are vital rhetorical material in *Stopping Traffic* because they become proxies for trafficking victims in order to create estimates. When prostitute figures appear in *Stopping Traffic,* they are there to advance the abolitionist policy position, which aims to eradicate the industry in which real prostitutes work.

Kelly and Regan do not explain the exclusion from their study of women engaged in off-street prostitution and women who migrated for marriage. They address only the absence of one group, admitting that it is "regrettable that neither the time nor resources available made possible gathering testimonies from trafficked women."[51] They profess that trafficking is illegal and hard to study. Left unsaid is that women engaged in off-street prostitution or migrating to marry have broken no laws in England and Wales.[52] The rationale of unreachability would not apply to these women; reaching them would not be like looking for needles in haystacks. In other words, these groups could be asked to participate as sources that inform the research. Nevertheless, *Stopping Traffic* is mum on what these women know about prostitution, trafficking, and migration, while making impactful claims about them and proposing policy that will directly affect them. Hence, targeted groups appear but are not heard in *Stopping Traffic,* a report speaking for prostitutes and migrants, who are often women.

Despite the methodological shortcomings of *Stopping Traffic,* Kelly and Regan conclude that the mix of "data sources, some more robust than others, suggests that the trafficking problem is of greater proportions, and located in many more cities and towns in the UK, than the known and confirmed cases suggest."[53] The report may look like scientific research, but it is abolitionist advocacy produced "to enable policy development."[54] Circulation of *Stopping Traffic*'s numbers, often the highest estimate in the range, by the government, police, media, and NGOs spoke to its acceptance as a reliable study. As I have shown, the material, methodology, and anti-prostitution ideology constituting *Stopping Traffic* evince that the first UK trafficking estimate was born bad.

---

50. A proxy is a figure that represents the value of something in a mathematical calculation.

51. Kelly and Regan, *Stopping Traffic,* 6.

52. In England and Wales, prostitution is legal when engaged in alone and indoors, but it is illegal to engage in street prostitution or work in a brothel or with others involved in prostitution, such as for example in the role of a receptionist. Migrating for marriage is also legal, but at the time, there was increasingly hostile rhetoric citing "sham" marriages between foreigners and citizens as a means of circumventing immigration restrictions.

53. Kelly and Regan, *Stopping Traffic,* 21.

54. Kelly and Regan, *Stopping Traffic,* 6.

But it got worse. Once the estimate of trafficked women was created, it took on a life of its own. The estimate was misrepresented and inflated when it traveled from the original report into new discursive contexts. Its rhetorical force persuaded policymakers and the public. The seductions of quantification made trafficking feel horribly real but also like a manageable problem. This twin effect galvanized UK antitrafficking efforts. The next section tracks the second UK estimate as momentum built for the national battle against *modern-day slavery.*

BUILDING ON A WEAK FOUNDATION: THE UK ESTIMATES TRAFFICKING, AGAIN

The United Nations Convention against Transnational Organized Crime tried to unify nations to fight organized crime by codifying new offenses, coordinating law enforcement, and building the crime-fighting capacity of national governments. Supplementing this convention, the Protocol to Prevent, Suppress and Punish Trafficking in Persons, Especially Women and Children served as the first legally binding international instrument to define trafficking. As the UN Office on Drugs and Crime explained,

> The intention behind this definition is to facilitate convergence in national
> approaches with regard to the establishment of domestic criminal offences
> that would support efficient international cooperation in investigating and
> prosecuting trafficking in persons cases. An additional objective of the Pro-
> tocol is to protect and assist the victims of trafficking in persons with full
> respect for their human rights.[55]

The protocol's primary aim was to criminalize trafficking through new laws at the national level combined with robust law enforcement. Its secondary aim was offering protection and assistance to trafficking victims. The primary and secondary aims index the tension between criminological and human rights approaches, because a human rights approach prioritizes victims of trafficking, whereas a criminological approach prioritizes prosecution and punishment, which can lead to the harmful effect of victims receiving protection in exchange for helping states with criminal cases. In practice, it

---

55. United Nations Office on Drugs and Crime, United Nations Convention against Transnational Organized Crime and the Protocols Thereto. Clearly, the protocol on trafficking is wide-ranging in its targets, yet the qualifier "Women and Children" indicates its focus on trafficking for sexual exploitation.

can be difficult to disentangle these approaches due to governments talking about victims' rights while detaining, prosecuting, and deporting women suspected of involvement in prostitution. Put another way, avowed human rights approaches manifest police responses. The UN added the human rights objective to the protocol to encourage governments to offer victims adequate support and safety.

The UK signed the convention in 2000, but it took until 2006 for it to enter into force. In the intervening years, the Labour government took steps to meet its convention obligations. One means to that end was estimating trafficking again. In 2003 the Home Office tapped economists, not feminist researchers, to draft a report. The shift in expertise might lead to an assumption that sound data and methods were used, thus improving upon *Stopping Traffic*. But as I detail below, the same mistakes and some new ones gave birth to another bad estimate.

Economists Richard Dubourg and Stephen Prichard coedited the fifty-one-page report, titled *The Impact of Organised Crime in the UK: Revenues and Economic and Social Costs*.[56] The report estimates the scale, revenue, and costs of organized crimes. It has chapters on people smuggling, people trafficking for sexual exploitation, illicit drugs, excise fraud, and other group-organized crimes. Criminal groups are defined as only "two or more persons, jointly engaged in continuing 'significant illegal activities,' irrespective of national or other boundaries."[57] They are also defined as capable of "violence, coercion, corruption or deception."[58] This definition is from the National Criminal Intelligence Service's 2003 UK Threat Assessment. Dubourg and Prichard further thank the "representatives of the Metropolitan Police Service, Operation REFLEX, NCIS and the numerous regional [police] forces" for their guidance and information contributing to the "people trafficking" chapter.[59]

Clearly, *The Impact of Organised Crime in the UK* measures a broad swath of organized crimes; however, like *Stopping Traffic*, it is preoccupied with trafficked women. Dubourg and a research team wrote the chapter titled

---

56. *The Impact of Organised Crime in the UK* was released with another report that focused on the criminal assets the UK could seize. The compilation of two reports was titled *Organised Crime: Revenues, Economic and Social Costs, and Criminal Assets Available for Seizure*. Since I focus on *The Impact of Organised Crime in the UK* report, I cite its title unless referring to the specific chapter on "People Trafficking." Each chapter was written by a different research team, but Dubourg and Prichard edited the report in its entirety.

57. Dubourg and Prichard, *Impact of Organised Crime*, 4. The National Criminal Intelligence Service (NCIS) merged with other units to form the Serious Organised Crime Agency (SOCA) in 2006.

58. Dubourg and Prichard, *Impact of Organised Crime*, 4.

59. Dubourg and Prichard, *Impact of Organised Crime*, i.

"People Trafficking for Sexual Exploitation," which uses the gender-neutral term "people" while estimating "trafficked women" only. They stress that the chapter "should be treated with great caution" and that its estimate is "very approximate."[60] But disclaimers aside, they justify estimating only *sex trafficking* by avowing, "there are no available data concerning other forms of people trafficking."[61] In 2007 a Home Office white paper echoed the idea that only women trafficked for sex could be estimated due to the lack of evidence about the agriculture, construction, domestic service, and food processing industries. The Home Office explained, "We do not have sufficient evidence regarding trafficking for forced labour to enable us to make a full assessment of whether it poses a significant problem for the UK."[62] Yet just ten pages later in that white paper, it acknowledged that "independent studies do suggest the existence of trafficking for forced labour / domestic servitude and also the existence of child trafficking."[63] In early reports, questions arose about what constituted enough evidence for creating estimates and conducting national threat assessments. Still, the Home Office accepted reports based on weak or nonexistent evidence. Dubious data was acceptable when estimating one form of trafficking but not others. That raises another question: Did panic over *sex trafficking* from East Europe drive the desire for numbers, any numbers?

My rhetorical-material analysis exposes how data (what, at times, it is even a stretch to call data) produced the first UK trafficking estimates. Although evidence existed on trafficking in industries outside of prostitution, that data was deemed insufficient for making estimates and evidence-based policy. Dismissing independent studies, the Home Office touted *The Impact of Organised Crime in the UK* as "ground breaking work."[64] Government faith in evidence seemed to rest on whether sex or labor trafficking was measured. Highlighting this tendency, the Home Office proclaimed, "Although the extent of [sex trafficking] is unclear, the evidence suggests that it is not reducing in either scale or reach."[65] Regarding labor trafficking, it lamented, "One of the difficulties we will face in investigating trafficking for forced labour is distinguishing between poor working conditions and situations involving forced labour."[66] Why the same thing could not be said about forced prostitution

---

60. Dubourg et al., "People Trafficking," 15. While estimating trafficked women only, the phrase "people trafficking" appears throughout the report, causing confusion when the estimate moved out of context.

61. Dubourg and Prichard, *Impact of Organised Crime*, 1.

62. Home Office, *UK Action Plan*, 5.

63. Home Office, *UK Action Plan*, 15.

64. Home Office, *UK Action Plan*, 20.

65. Home Office, *UK Action Plan*, 20.

66. Home Office, *UK Action Plan*, 5.

goes unexplained, as if that distinction is obvious. Voicing its qualms about telling the difference between labor trafficking and everyday exploitation, the UK government turned prostitution into an easy target.

Seduced by Specificity:
From Estimate Ranges to an Exact Number

Much as Kelly and Regan did in *Stopping Traffic*, Dubourg and the team authoring the chapter on "People Trafficking for Sexual Exploitation" made prostitutes into proxies. But unlike Kelly and Regan, they reject estimate ranges since "there is little to base any ranges on, and there is a danger they would falsely indicate that the degree of uncertainty could be quantified precisely."[67] To avoid quantifying uncertainty, they quash it with a precise number. That rhetorical strategy misleads, however, because it implies precision instead of uncertainty. Making matters worse, Dubourg et al. explain that the "methodology for estimating the number of victims in London is driven largely by the analysis contained in Dickson."[68] This reference is to a report, *Sex in the City: Mapping Commercial Sex across London*, by Sandra Dickson and the Poppy Project, which was a London-based service provider for trafficked women. *Sex in the City* intended to "clarify the scale and range of venues selling sex, and therefore the numbers of women working in prostitution."[69] According to Dubourg et al., for sources it used "free local newspapers, internet sex guides, [i]nternet advertisements and so on" to calculate "the number of establishments selling sex."[70] It estimated the number of prostitutes at each establishment based on information in the ads and what it called "informed judgements."[71] Through this method, *Sex in the City* posited 6,405 women working in London's off-street prostitution sector.

And again like Regan and Kelly, researchers rely on a *Times* news story as a data source. Headlined "Albanians Take Over Organised Crime," the story says, "In towns and cities across Britain last night members of the oldest profession were working for a new and sinister breed of employer."[72] Using dehumanizing terms, the story amplifies the idea of East European criminal gangs running a traffic in women, thereby overdetermining Albanian migrants as

---

67. Dubourg and Prichard, *Impact of Organised Crime*, 2.
68. Dubourg et al., "People Trafficking," 16.
69. Dickson and the Poppy Project, *Sex in the City*, 5.
70. Dubourg et al., "People Trafficking," 16.
71. Dubourg et al., "People Trafficking," 16.
72. Cobain, "Albanians Take Over Organised Crime."

TABLE 1. Number of sex workers in London by establishment

ESTABLISHMENT	SOURCE	ESTIMATED NUMBER OF WOMEN INVOLVED IN PROSTITUTION IN LONDON
Flats, saunas and massage parlours	Midpoint of range estimated by Dickson	4,417
Escort agencies	Midpoint of range estimated by Dickson	1,988
Walk-ups	*The Times*	420
Total		6,825

Source: Dubourg et al., "People Trafficking," 16.

evil criminals. Consistent with trafficking discourse in the news media, it com-
plements sensational claims with an official estimate: "Scotland Yard estimates
that Albanian gangs control about 75 per cent of prostitution in Soho. Many
of the women and children caught up in the trade are the victims of a modern
form of slavery, kidnapped or tricked into coming to Britain."[73] Dubourg et al.
cite this story as reporting an estimated seventy walk-up establishments used
for prostitution in London. That detail is not in the online version of the story,
but the researchers employ it to estimate 420 women in walk-ups, assuming
six women in each establishment. The number 70 appears in the online story
but as a *percentage.* The online version reads, "Albanians control over 70 per
cent of Soho vice and send £12 million a year back to Albania from the earn-
ings of about 1,000 women." It also reports, "Albanian gangs control about
75 per cent of prostitution in Soho." In this context, the word "vice" refers to
prostitution, meaning the story gives different percentages for the same thing:
"over 70 per cent Soho vice" and "about 75 per cent of prostitution in Soho."
While "about 75 per cent" is "over 70 per cent," the loose use of statistics in this
story makes it a poor choice for a data source. As does the rhetorical slippage
from impugning "Albanian gangs" to "Albanians" as a whole.

In total, one NGO report and one news story form the basis for Dubourg
et al.'s estimate of London sex workers, on which they will extrapolate to come
up with an estimate of trafficked women in the UK. In table 1, I reproduce their
table of estimate ranges based on the two sources. Despite the earlier criticism
that estimate ranges "falsely indicate" that "the degree of uncertainty could be
quantified precisely," the analysis relies on ranges and, in their words, "simply takes the midpoint of these ranges."[74] Consequently, while their estimate

---

73. Cobain, "Albanians Take Over Organised Crime."
74. Dubourg et al., "People Trafficking," 16.

TABLE 2. Assumptions regarding proportion trafficked in London

ESTABLISHMENT	PROPORTION THAT ARE OF FOREIGN ORIGIN	OF WOMEN THAT ARE OF FOREIGN ORIGIN, PROPORTION SMUGGLED	OF WOMEN THAT ARE SMUGGLED, ASSUMED PROPORTION TRAFFICKED	ESTIMATED NUMBER OF TRAFFICKED WOMEN IN LONDON
Flats, etc.	80%	50%	75%	1,325
Escort agencies	80%	20%	10%	32
Walk-ups	90%	100%	100%	378

Source: Dubourg et al., "People Trafficking," 17. We might recall that the health project workers mentioned in *Stopping Traffic* claimed that 5 percent of migrant prostitutes in London were trafficked. Although it was unclear if that percentage referred to on- or off-street prostitution, or both sectors, the gulf between that figure and Dubourg et al.'s much larger percentages should give pause.

of trafficked women may not be expressed as a range, it is constructed from ranges that become concealed in the final figure.

From this estimate of London off-street sex workers, Dubourg and coauthors move to calculate how many are trafficked, explaining their method as follows:

> First, the number of women who are of foreign origin is estimated and of these women, informed assumptions about how many are trafficked are made. This enables a calculation of the total number of trafficked workers in London, split by establishment. The assumptions concerning flats, saunas and massage parlours are based on discussions with CO14 [Metropolitan Police Clubs and Vice Unit], and the researchers assume that all foreign workers in walk-ups are trafficked.[75]

Jumping from the huge assumption, among others, that *foreign* equals *forced* at a rate of 100 percent in walk-ups, they construct another table (see table 2) with percentages focusing on foreign women and the mode of entry into sex work.

Walking readers through the method, they announce, "The next step is to extrapolate to the full UK market, where data are even weaker."[76] To perform the extrapolation, as their third source, they turn to a regional guidebook that reviews commercial sex venues and sex workers. "It is possible to derive from *The McCoy's British Massage Parlour Guide* an estimate of the total number of women involved in prostitution in the UK," they note, "but this is unlikely to

75. Dubourg et al., "People Trafficking," 16.
76. Dubourg et al., "People Trafficking," 17.

be comprehensive—the researchers judge that Dickson's estimates for London are more reliable than those derived from assessing McCoy's."[77] Dubourg et al. do not explain why they judge Dickson's estimates to be more reliable than *McCoy's*, but these sources sit at opposite ends of the ideological spectrum. On one end, Eaves Housing for Women is a London charity committed to abolishing prostitution; it set up the Poppy Project and produced the *Sex in the City* report. On the other end, George McCoy's guidebook ranks venues offering sexual services and the women who work in them.

Eaves Housing for Women set up the Poppy Project in 2003 after receiving £2.4 million from the Home Office to assist women trafficked for sexual exploitation. As the single NGO to receive such funding in the UK, the Poppy Project offered support services and allocated nine beds in the capital city for trafficked women.[78] Meanwhile, Eaves also conducted research and lobbied the government. Noting this NGO-government alliance, public policy scholar Belinda Brooks-Gordon remarked, "The Home Office gives money to the Poppy project, which in turn lobbies the government. If this sounds rather circular, it is."[79] That circularity had a startling arc. The Poppy Project produced the *Sex in the City* report, one of the primary sources for Dubourg et al.'s trafficking estimate, which the government cited to justify its antitrafficking agenda, which funded the Poppy Project. That financial arrangement carried on until the Salvation Army won the service contract in 2011. The Conservative-led coalition government giving a £4 million contract to a Christian organization "immediately prompted a campaign by luminaries such as Professor Liz Kelly, the chair of the End Violence Against Women Coalition, and urgent appeals for donations to help the [Poppy] project continue supporting victims of trafficking."[80] Millions in funds were at stake when the government brokered antitrafficking alliances with NGOs—an unusual prospect for a problem framed as gender-based violence.[81]

---

77. Dubourg et al., "People Trafficking," 17.

78. The small number of beds raises questions: Why only nine beds when the UK government and the Poppy Project claimed trafficking was a big problem? Why were beds located just in London if trafficking was happening across the country? In a way, the nine beds aligned with trafficking rhetoric, since it targeted *sex trafficking*, and the beds were for women, excluding other victims and forms of trafficking from state-funded services and lodging.

79. Brooks-Gordon, "Red Mist."

80. Townsend, "Sex-Trafficked Women's Charity."

81. This antitrafficking alliance resonates with Elizabeth Bernstein's influential observation about the "strange bedfellows," that is, US abolitionist feminists and evangelical Christians, who found common ground on the issue of human trafficking. See Bernstein, "Militarized Humanitarianism Meets Carceral Feminism."

Contrary to the abolitionist position, the *McCoy's* guidebook publicized sexual services. Judging the two sources, Dubourg and coauthors write, "Dickson estimates that there are 6,405 sex workers in off-street brothels and escort agencies in London, compared with an equivalent figure of 1,420 derived from examining McCoy's."[82] The number from *McCoy's* is, incredibly, the same as the maximum figure in Kelly and Regan's estimate range (1,420).[83] Dubourg et al. think that *McCoy's* underestimates the number of prostitutes, so they raise its estimate, arriving at the very precise-sounding figure of 3,812 trafficked women in the UK in 2003.

Unveiling the new number, Dubourg et al. add more caveats to the disclaimers given in the report's introduction. Aware of the potential comparisons with *Stopping Traffic*, they warn, "This total estimate should *not* be directly compared with the range of 142 and 1,420 quoted in Kelly and Regan" because Kelly and Regan estimated "the *flow* of victims trafficked in 1998," whereas *The Impact of Organised Crime in the UK* estimated "the *stock* of victims trafficked (in 2003)."[84] They insist that the higher estimate "presents no evidence concerning whether the scale of people trafficking has fallen or risen since 1998."[85] They also concede, for a second time, that the estimate "was not directly informed by evidence concerning the number of women observed to have been trafficked."[86] Ultimately, the "people trafficking" estimate is not based on evidence or observation of the people it claimed to count. The method boils down to using derivative data from discrepant sources. Much like *Stopping Traffic*, assumptions about prostitutes and migrant women guide the calculation. In both cases, the UK government solicited estimates of trafficking in order to develop policy and policing strategies. The two estimates can be compared in terms of their creation and circulation. Thus far in this chapter, I have covered the birth of the UK's initial trafficking estimates. In the next section, I track the rhetorical life of Dubourg et al.'s estimate as it traveled out of its original context, to illustrate how media coverage both cited the estimate and quickly ballooned beyond it. Circulating the figures vouched for *sex trafficking* in the UK which, in turn, substantiated repressive state responses.

---

82. Dubourg et al., "People Trafficking," 17.

83. To my knowledge, it is a coincidence that the number is exactly the same as *Stopping Traffic's* maximum figure. Dubourg et al. make no comment about the coincidence. It should be clear that neither *Stopping Traffic* nor *McCoy's* contains reliable data for creating official estimates.

84. Dubourg et al., "People Trafficking," 18.

85. Dubourg et al., "People Trafficking," 18.

86. Dubourg et al., "People Trafficking," 18.

Speculative Figures in the Media:
How Estimates Went from Bad to Worse

Journalist Nick Davies criticized the circulation of misinformation about human trafficking in the UK. He wrote that estimates of trafficking were

> stripped of caution, stretched to their most alarming possible meaning and tossed into the public domain. There, they have been picked up by the media who have stretched them even further in stories which have been treated as reliable sources by politicians, who in turn provided quotes for more misleading stories.[87]

This media trend is evident in the rampant distortion of Dubourg et al.'s estimate. Taken out of context, the 3,812 trafficked women estimate traveled without the data and method that created it. When the antitrafficking operation Pentameter 2 was being covered by the media in 2007, Dr. Tim Brain, the chief constable of Gloucestershire and gold commander of Pentameter 2, declared that "a large proportion of the estimated 4,000 trafficked women and men forced into prostitution worked in residential houses and flats in towns and even villages across Britain."[88] Erroneously, Brain includes men in Dubourg et al.'s estimate. Another 2007 news story reported, "The Home Office believes the number of illegal immigrants being sexually exploited at any one time is about 4,000."[89] Stretching the 2003 estimate to a perpetual number existing "at any one time," it uses the term "illegal immigrants" as the estimate's referent group. As detailed earlier, Dubourg et al. used estimates of prostitutes as proxies to estimate trafficked women. Moreover, trafficked women were supposed to be seen as victims of crime, not as "illegal immigrants." Enlarging the estimate, the story continues, "Investigators and support groups, however, calculate numbers are likely to be in excess of 10,000 and describe known cases as the 'tip of the iceberg.'"[90] This casts doubt on the government's estimate but only to suggest that it is too small. The real number must be bigger, so a titanic figure *more than double* the official estimate is given without explanation or a direct source.

A 2008 story in *The Guardian* surpassed the 10,000 estimate when reporting that the "latest estimates by police suggest there could be as many as 18,000

---

87. Davies, "Prostitution and Trafficking."
88. Travis, "Sex Trafficking Victims Rescued."
89. Townsend, "'Sex Slaves' Win Cash."
90. Townsend, "'Sex Slaves' Win Cash."

trafficking victims being forced to work as prostitutes in the UK."[91] Another *Guardian* story from that same year exceeded all the numbers when declaring, "Metropolitan police have estimated that 70% of the 88,000 women involved in prostitution in England and Wales are under the control of traffickers."[92] To put this percentage into perspective, it would mean that traffickers controlled more than 67,000 women in England and Wales, but a few years earlier, the official estimate was 3,812 trafficked women for the entire UK. The popularity of 70 percent as a go-to guesstimate appears again, like it did in *The Times* article that Dubourg et. al used as a source.

In a short time span, mainstream media outlets circulated trafficking estimates, ranging from 4,000 to 67,000, for everchanging referent populations and regions. These figures suggest that the presence of estimates mattered more than numerical accuracy in the news. As I argue in the chapter's introduction, the impossibility of arriving at an accurate number allowed estimates to proliferate and persuade, which illustrates how speculative figures rhetorically constituted the problem they appeared to measure. By incorporating anti-prostitution abolitionist ideology in the seemingly objective domain of quantification, estimates became warrants for state action, amply underscored by the police spokespeople giving numbers to the media. Trafficking estimates were taken from their original contexts, inflated, and circulated free from details about their reliability and provenance. In this discursive circuit, speculative and wildly fluctuating figures corroborated speculative and wildly fluctuating claims about trafficking in the UK.

The media communicated trafficking rhetoric in the captivating form of sensational "sex slave" stories and speculative estimates. Media coverage hyped the UK antitrafficking strategy. An antitrafficking assemblage among state, media, and NGOs developed when *Stopping Traffic* recommended that the government appoint an NGO to help victims of trafficking. The Labour government picked the Poppy Project to offer support services and shelter for trafficked women, and it produced research such as the *Sex in the City* study that Dubourg and colleagues relied on to create their estimate of trafficked women. Anti-prostitution abolitionist ideology generated the nascent UK antitrafficking agenda by running through the state-media-NGO circuit. Before I end this chapter, I want to bring up a critical moment when the state-media-NGO circuit surfaced and created a controversy, which was significant because there was scant public discussion about the powerful alliances forged through the UK antitrafficking agenda.

---

91. Williams, "British-Born Teenagers Being Trafficked."
92. Travis and Sparrow, "New Law to Criminalize Men."

In 2008 journalist Julie Bindel and a Poppy Project staffer, Helen Atkins, published *Big Brothel: A Survey of the Off-Street Sex Industry in London* as the follow-up to *Sex in the City*.[93] If *Sex in the City* mapped off-street prostitution, then *Big Brothel* filled in the map by cataloging sexual services, prices, workers, and workplaces. A covert phone survey was used to obtain data. Men pretending to be prospective clients called brothels to ask questions to whomever picked up the phone. The responses were collected as evidence about sexual services, prices, workers, and workplaces. A covert phone survey alone cannot provide reliable data, and the anti-prostitution slant is evident in the report's language as well as its methodology. In *Big Brothel*'s foreword, Denise Marshall OBE, chief executive officer of Eaves, announces, "Nowhere is the inequality more stark than in the case of prostitution, where the roles of women and men are constructed as fundamentally different, in ways that support and maintain gender inequality."[94] Her claim is followed by a bulleted list of binary oppositions, which readers are meant to attach to men and women: "Buyer/bought, Sex drive/sexual object, Hunter/prey."[95]

Pushing this viewpoint, *Big Brothel* misrepresented prostitution as cheap and dangerous to public health. Under the heading "What's on the Menu in London's Brothels?" a page that resembles a restaurant menu declares, "Kissing, oral or anal sex without a condom for an extra tenner."[96] The page displays a list of findings, implying that £10 is a typical upcharge. But the report states that only 2 percent of the brothels surveyed by phone claimed to offer unprotected penetrative sex. It says the price for unprotected oral or anal sex ranged from £10 to £200, with an average of £71.25.[97] Whereas with trafficking estimates the *highest* number in the range is highlighted, the *lowest* price is put on this menu, which also conflates the health risks of kissing and unprotected sex. While *Big Brothel* offers an admission "that the source data contains some misleading information," its lurid presentation negates its pretense of reliable material.[98]

---

93. Bindel and Atkins, *Big Brothel*. Like *Sex in the City*, this title plays on the name of a popular television show, the reality TV series *Big Brother* (which, unlike the US show *Sex in the City*, had a British version of the same name).

94. Bindel and Atkins, *Big Brothel*, ii. The honorific OBE, which stands for the Most Excellent Order of the British Empire, is one of the rewards given by the British sovereign to citizens for contributions to the arts and science, charity, or public service.

95. Bindel and Atkins, *Big Brothel*, ii.

96. Bindel and Atkins, *Big Brothel*, 4.

97. Bindel and Atkins, *Big Brothel*, 4. Given the dubious method of data collection, the report's claims about pricing are not credible.

98. Bindel and Atkins, *Big Brothel*, 5.

The *Big Brothel* menu gave media outlets preselected sound bites that would cause alarm. Additionally, to promote the report, Bindel wrote a *Guardian* article titled "Revealed: The Truth about Brothels." In it, she claimed, "What Big Brothel shows is that commercial sex is becoming as normalised as stopping off for a McDonald's."[99] Like Kelly and Regan's claim to reveal the "true scale" of trafficking, Bindel too lays claim to truth. As intended, *Big Brothel*'s speculative figures drummed up media attention and public outcry about prostitution. A coalition of twenty-seven academics composed a detailed response to *Big Brothel* that criticized its lack of rigor and ethical procedure. The response opens with their apprehensions not only about the content of the report but also the media and public consumption of it:

> We are worried about the salacious nature of the report and the media "hype" that has been generated regarding the safer sexual practices and the price of sexual services in the UK. Due to considerable media attention and exposure given to the report, there is the danger of misrepresentations impacting upon very important social and public policy issues.[100]

Amid growing pressure, the Poppy Project distanced itself from the controversy. It maintained that *Big Brothel* was not an academic study and that the media received a link to the full report with the menu. Yet the Poppy Project also indicated that the media coverage of *Big Brothel* was an end unto itself, because, it alleged, the media favored the sex industry:

> It is rare for a report such as Big Brothel to achieve significant media coverage, and it is essential in the interests of furthering the debate to provide a counter-balance to the disproportionately positive media focus on prostitution enjoyed by those who substantially profit from the sex industry, such as pornographers, brothel owners and lap dance clubs.[101]

The Poppy Project also clarified that the antitrafficking funding it received did not go toward the production of *Big Brothel*. At best, however, the Poppy Project published a misleading study on prostitution while it was the only NGO receiving government funds to assist trafficked women.

---

99. Bindel, "Revealed: The Truth about Brothels."

100. Sanders et al., *Academic Response to "Big Brothel."*

101. Poppy Project, *POPPY Project's Comments in Response to "Academics."* The scare quotes around the word "Academics" aim to cast doubt on the credentials and credibility of the twenty-seven scholars and researchers criticizing *Big Brothel.*

CONCLUSION

In this chapter, I detailed how estimates of prostitutes and an assortment of other sources, based on dubious material and methods, laid the foundation for the first trafficking estimates in the UK. As quantitative rhetoric, the estimates influenced law, policy, policing, and public perceptions by furnishing the UK government with what looked like empirical grounds for targeting prostitution and presenting antitrafficking strategies as necessary to stop an evil and transnational crime. But *Stopping Traffic* and *The Impact of Organised Crime in the UK* did not offer objective measures or reflections of reality in the form of numbers. These speculative figures were made to persuade policymakers and the public about the exigency of human trafficking, framed as forced migration and prostitution. While it is possible to create estimates of well-defined social phenomena, as this chapter reveals, the UK trafficking estimates had the sheen of empiricism without the substance. A rhetorical-material analysis parses how bad numbers are created and circulated ostensibly for a good cause. The representation of trafficking estimates as trustworthy enabled a contestable ideological position on prostitution to appear neutral while pursuing a repressive criminological agenda targeting prostitutes and migrants. The desire for data-driven, evidence-based governance means that estimates play a vital role in substantiating state projects. Rhetorical-material analysis affords an incisive method for tracking quantitative discourse's emergence and effects.

Official numbers communicate that a problem exists, the government is measuring it, and the public must be made aware of it. The next chapter analyzes the *UK Action Plan on Tackling Human Trafficking,* the government white paper that used Dubourg et al.'s estimate to bolster its national antitrafficking strategy. In taking up the *Action Plan,* I chronicle and challenge how the UK peddled speculative figures and a false history of abolition to realize a state agenda premised on remembering and forgetting the transatlantic slave trade.

CHAPTER 2

Anti-Blackness by Analogy

Human Trafficking as Modern-Day Slavery

After the European Union expanded in 2004 and 2007, the United Kingdom shifted to a closed-door policy toward East Europeans, pointing to trafficking as a reason for imposing immigration restrictions. As chapter 1 covered, the antitrafficking agenda was unveiled in the *UK Action Plan on Tackling Human Trafficking* in 2007. The white paper venerated Britain abolishing the slave trade in 1807, while announcing that the UK was ready to revive the abolitionist mission to fight *modern-day slavery.* For rhetoric scholar Stephen H. Browne, the commemoration of events is pedagogical in that it brings the past to the collective mind and teaches the public to remember in a particular way.[1] In this instance, the bicentenary forms an occasion to recall Britain's history of abolition, restating the event in a way that extols British values and vision. As heritage scholars Emma Waterton and Ross Wilson note, the bicentennial commemoration "works to move Britain away from the politically fraught arena of apology and reparation, while simultaneously firming up the role of Britain as a *leading* player" in abolition.[2] To fabricate the national self-image, the bicentenary celebrates Britain by stage-managing its *leading* role in slave trading so that it does not tarnish the UK. Spotlighting British benevolence toward enslaved peoples, the bicentenary distances Britain from the slave

---

1. Browne, "Remembering Crispus Attucks."
2. Waterton and Wilson, "Talking the Talk," 386.

trade but tightens the link between abolition and antitrafficking. In a performative flourish signaling that linkage, Home Secretary John Reid signed the Council of Europe Convention on Action against Trafficking, on what was once William Wilberforce's desk, in 2007.[3]

How Britain recollects its past informs claims about its present and future. As this chapter unpacks, the tactical handling of history to frame new policy indexes the racial logics alive in the UK's bicentennial celebration of abolition and antitrafficking agenda, and how these projects are conjoined. Rhetoric scholar Robert Asen explains, "As policies mediate rhetorical and material elements, the process of policymaking foregrounds the role of rhetoric as a constitutive force."[4] In the same vein, political scientist and policy scholar Erin O'Brien argues, "the repetition of a singular, or dominant, narrative can have significant, and damaging, implications on policy."[5] Taking my cue from Asen and O'Brien, I analyze the constitutive force of rhetoric, particularly the modern-day slavery narrative, that wrought the UK's antitrafficking policymaking.

Trafficking rhetoric participates in the bicentennial recollection of abolition by using it to assert that the UK must now defeat a new slave trade. Trafficking rhetoric produces a discursive situation in which the afterlives of transatlantic slavery go unaddressed, while the term "modern-day slavery" is incessantly invoked. Moreover, it produces a discursive situation where the UK government addresses how to control immigrants (while appearing to talk about something else) and contain immigration (while appearing to target something else). According to Sara Ahmed, "Immigration is a useful narrative because it is about race [but appears] not to be about race."[6] Trafficking is also a useful narrative because it is about race, immigration, and national identity, but antitrafficking advocates make it appear detached from those controversial things. Recall the NGO executive, quoted in the book's introduction, who worried that trafficking was "tarnished" when connected to immigration.

By contrast, policy analyst Jacqueline Berman argues that concerns about trafficking are "a constitutive part of border issues," which enable states to

---

3. Balch, "Defeating 'Modern Slavery,'" 79. Wilberforce was an English politician who led the decades-long parliamentary campaign against Britain's slave trade. Critics of the government's celebration of the bicentenary, specifically its focus on white men, dubbed it "Wilberfest." The Council of Europe Convention on Action against Trafficking in Human Beings is the full title; this treaty entered into force in 2008, and it is notable for its focus on human rights and victim protection.

4. Asen, "Reflections on the Role of Rhetoric," 129.

5. O'Brien, *Challenging the Human Trafficking Narrative*, 3.

6. Ahmed, "Bogus."

"claim control over the border and perform the role of 'securer' of the nation."[7]
Since population displacement and state processes of illegalizing immigrants
"are represented as problems of trafficking," according to sociologist Nandita
Sharma, "a particular 'solution' comes to make common sense: criminalize
those who move people clandestinely and return those who have been moved
by traffickers to their 'home' societies."[8] The *Action Plan* promotes a criminological solution as common sense for tackling trafficking risks for particular populations and protecting the UK from serious organized crime. Once
attached to crime and border control, trafficking rhetoric underwrites a plan
to secure the nation, specifically by containing immigration. Immigration is
claimed to cloak trafficking and compromise Britain, which must be defended
from slavery's sudden arrival. National insecurity is thus blamed on seemingly
uncontrolled immigration—a fear that eventually helped to secure the referendum vote in 2016 for the UK to exit the EU.

The *Action Plan* defines trafficking as a threat to national security, but, I
argue, trafficking rhetoric manufactures material and symbolic borders while
promoting a climate of hostility that threatens immigrants and marginalized
UK citizens. To show how the government's veneration of abolition shores up
state action against immigrants, I examine the *Action Plan*'s paradoxical solution to trafficking. The *Action Plan* produces a paradox because the EU is premised on the Four Freedoms: the free movement of goods, services, capital,
and people. This principle means that EU citizens ought to be able to work,
reside, and travel in EU member states without facing discrimination, because
they are treated like domestic citizens. To be sure, this principle was not real-
ized by most EU states in relation to the accession of East and Central European countries in 2004 and 2007. For my purposes in this chapter, I focus on
how, by linking East Europeans' migration to trafficking, the UK antitrafficking agenda and the *Action Plan* in particular, turned EU citizens into policy
targets ostensibly to defend the UK border and labor market.

Analyzing textual and visual depictions of East Europeans, literary studies scholar Anca Parvulescu explains how racialization suggests that "occu-
pational positions, religious markers, and issues and debates (immigration,
criminality) have become imbued with racial meanings that are variable, often
contradictory, and differentially applied."[9] East European people living in the
UK experience stratification and stigmatization (for example, stereotypes of
the "Polish plumber" and "Natasha prostitute") that racialize their locations
in the labor market. Whiteness is conjured contradictorily to represent East

---

7. Berman, "(Un)Popular Strangers and Crises (Un)Bounded," 50.
8. Sharma, "Anti-Trafficking Rhetoric," 89.
9. Parvulescu, *Traffic in Women's Work*, 14.

Europeans as either modern slaves or economic migrants, with both classifications claimed to cost the UK money and to cause Britishness to lose its value. The sociologist Robert Miles, as Parvulescu reminds us, introduced a concept of racialization "to describe the situation of migrant workers in Britain in the twentieth century."[10] Interrogating the EU supranational scheme to soften borders among member states, philosopher Rosi Braidotti calls for analysis of the "new racialized hierarchy that polices access to full EU citizenship" to map the "new forms of 'othering' that are made operational as a result of EU enlargement."[11] I contend that UK trafficking rhetoric functioned to "other" or "alienize" East Europeans during a time of unprecedented EU expansion.[12] I therefore track trafficking rhetoric to map how East EU citizens came to be racialized as threats to British values and national security.

This chapter argues that the *Action Plan* produces a racialized hierarchy to police access to the UK and its labor market by (1) invoking the transatlantic slave trade and abolition to make trafficking and the UK antitrafficking agenda legible and (2) visualizing white people as human trafficking's victims. The racialized hierarchy constituted through trafficking rhetoric stigmatizes East Europeans by discursively tying them to *modern-day slavery* while sidelining how Black people, the victims of transatlantic slavery, still live with its legacy. At the same time, trafficking rhetoric portrays slavery as anathema to the core British values of freedom, justice, and equality. Sociologist Julia O'Connell Davidson notes that the narrative of trafficking does not recognize people's desire to migrate but instead focuses on stopping their movement. Acknowledging that desire, O'Connell Davidson writes, "moves us onto much more difficult and contested political territory: that of state control over human mobility."[13] To rail against slavery in the twenty-first century produces a rhetoric with little risk of opposition, and the benefits that come from political consensus. It articulates an argument that no one can argue against, by tying migration to crime—the worst kind of crime—perpetrated by foreign others. Trafficking rhetoric thus silences critique because discursive positions are consigned to being for or against slavery, which is a formidable argumentative terrain that occludes structural and affective factors shaping migration. Restricting discursive and geographical borders, the UK government reacts forcefully not to the enslavement of others but to the insecurity and uncertain propagation of Britishness.

---

10. Parvulescu, *Traffic in Women's Work*, 15.

11. Braidotti, "On Becoming Europeans," 34.

12. See Chávez's book *The Borders of AIDS* for a theory of the alienizing logics of citizenship in the US context.

13. O'Connell Davidson, *Modern Slavery*, 112.

COMMEMORATIVE COINS AND BROKEN CHAINS: ANTITRAFFICKING ANALOGIES

As chapter 1 discussed, the UN Protocol to Prevent, Suppress and Punish Trafficking in Persons, Especially Women and Children required signatory states to criminalize trafficking but left it to national governments to devise their own unique approaches. The Labour government rolled out an antitrafficking agenda after signing the protocol in 2000, which entered into force in 2006 in the UK. Since the protocol's main objective was the national-level criminalization of trafficking, the *UK Action Plan on Tackling Human Trafficking* aimed to realize that purpose after the Home Office and Scottish Executive undertook a national consultation for proposals on how to address trafficking. In what follows, I analyze the *Action Plan*'s textual and visual rhetoric, paying close attention to the two constitutive analogies that anchor the plan and represent migrants as modern-day slaves. Trafficking is analogized to transatlantic slavery, and antitrafficking is analogized to abolition. To disentangle this discursive web, I analyze the *Action Plan*'s cover page, foreword, executive summary, and a full-page poster in the document. Querying official claims that slavery arrived from elsewhere in the form of the foreigner, I exhibit how the racialized identity of *slave* sustains a national security project premised on xenophobic exclusion and Anglo ethnic pride.

The *Action Plan* cover page bears a hallmark with an exergue that reads, "Reflecting on the Past, Looking to the Future" (see figure 3). In the hallmark's center, zeroes in the numerals expressing the two years, 1807 and 2007, are linked by a representation of a chain, drawing an explicit visual connection between the 2007 *Action Plan* and the 1807 Slave Trade Act. Making graphic analogical links, the UK depicts its antitrafficking agenda as a moral intervention to stop an evil crime.

The analogical linking of transatlantic slavery and trafficking also materialized in 2007 as legal tender when an image akin to the *Action Plan* hallmark—1807 with a manacle and the words "An Act for the Abolition of the Slave Trade"—was embossed on £2 coins (see figure 4). The coin's obverse bore the crowned profile of Queen Elizabeth II, and the inscription along its edge reads, "Am I Not a Man and a Brother." This rhetorical question comes from the past; it accompanied an infamous eighteenth-century abolitionist image depicting a naked, kneeling African man in chains beseeching a white audience to bestow freedom upon him. Oblivious to the crushing irony of using currency to commemorate abolition, this antislavery token is put to work to promote the UK antitrafficking agenda. Thus, a white paper and commemorative coin illustrate trafficking rhetoric's circulation of a celebratory narrative

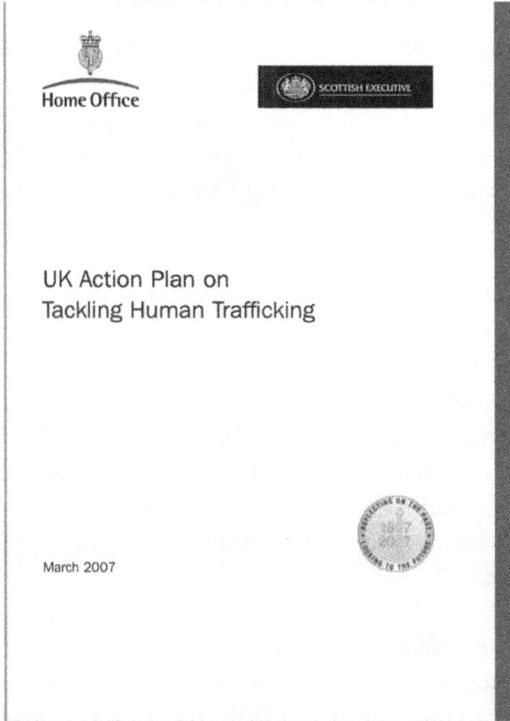

FIGURE 3. *UK Action Plan on Tackling Human Trafficking* front cover.

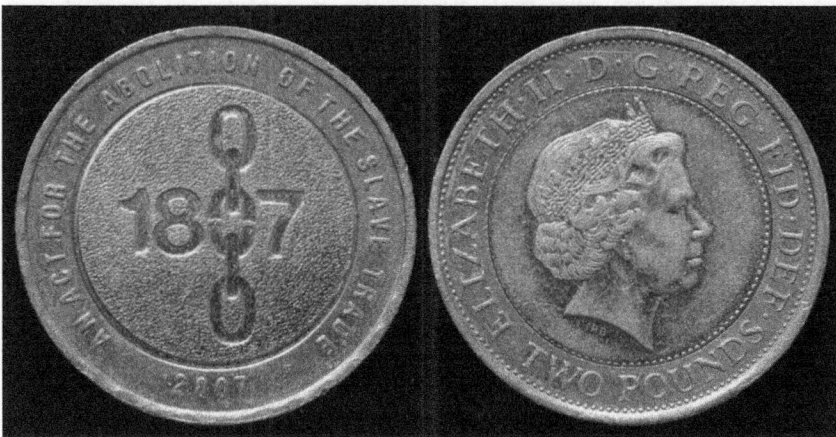

FIGURE 4. 2007 commemorative abolition coin. Used with permission from Matthew Weber.

about Britain liberating slaves. To secure British cultural and financial capital, a severed connection between the past and present is imagined as one year, centuries ago, bisected by a broken chain.

Building on the imagined link between slavery and trafficking, the *Action Plan* fleshes out this visual rhetoric of trafficking. Authoring the foreword, Home Secretary John Reid and Scottish Executive Minister for Justice Cathy Jamieson declare:

> Trafficking in human beings is an abhorrent crime. Many describe it as modern-day slavery, where victims are coerced, deceived or forced into the control of others who crudely and inhumanely seek to profit from their suffering. This year, it is 200 years since Parliament passed the Act to abolish the slave trade in the British Empire. Whilst we reflect on the past with the numerous events planned to mark the bicentenary, we must not forget the plight of the thousands of people who are still forced to live in slave like conditions as a result of the inhuman criminal practices perpetrated by 21st century traffickers.[14]

Note the use of the adjective "inhuman," rather than inhumane. The word choice is telling in that it highlights British humanism and commitment to human rights, even for traffickers.[15] It draws on what sociologist Eduardo Bonilla-Silva terms "modern-day *cultural racism*" as it conjures the image of a civilized nation fighting a brutal Other who originates from elsewhere.[16] In this way, the foreword presents the main figures in the fight for freedom: victims of trafficking reduced to enslavement, traffickers reduced to criminals engaging in "inhuman" practices, and the state enlarged by its abolitionist role. Charting a direct line from 1807 to 2007, the foreword describes the UK as heir to abolition and in possession of a historical remit to vanquish slavery. The *Action Plan*'s executive summary echoes this historical account and call to action:

> This year marks the bicentenary of the legal abolition of the slave trade in the former British Empire. Whilst a number of events are taking place to commemorate this event, we are faced with another challenge 200 years after the slave trade was legally abolished—how we tackle trafficking in human

14. Home Office, *UK Action Plan*, 2.
15. The United Nations Human Rights Council and the Anti-Trafficking Monitoring Group accused the UK government of violating human rights and the rule of law when implementing antitrafficking policies and policing.
16. Bonilla-Silva, "Invisible Weight of Whiteness," 179.

beings and the misery that it causes. This modern form of slavery is an evil practice perpetrated for profit with no regard for the personal or societal consequences. We are committed to tackling this crime and addressing the harms caused.[17]

The selective memory invoking abolition in effect anchors the *Action Plan* to a singular event—a moment of abolition—and links it to antitrafficking policy. The temporal containment enacted by this rhetoric induces what Stuart Hall terms "historical amnesia," which recalls the abolition of the slave trade but erases slavery's piecemeal demolition.[18] The imperial claims and iron chains on Black bodies were not broken by a pen stroke. Despite this historical fact, trafficking rhetoric fashions the British Empire as the site that abolished the slave trade, rather than as the heart of a system amassing the industry, corporations, and capital to organize and sustain a global trade in people. Further, this partial way of remembering and celebrating abolition also credits the UK as exceptionally suited to tackling trafficking due to its prior success ending its own slave trade.

Asserting an abolitionist knack is dubious because the Slave Trade Act passed after three centuries of slaving, but Britain did excel at enslavement. Britain's long history of slaving could therefore position it as exceptionally suited to apprehending the strategies of people who enslave others to enrich themselves. British history could also direct attention to migration. The multicentury slave trade took place when British subjects traveled across the globe in search of land, labor, and markets. Instead, in trafficking rhetoric, references to slavery and abolition operate to define an evil crime and to declare freedom, justice, and equality as uniquely British values, in the past and present. By contrast, to remember British exploits in other lands would expose the paradox of an antitrafficking plan predicated on restricting immigration and making it hard for people to move safely, legally, and without the assistance of third parties.

In the eighteenth and nineteenth centuries, abolition debates galvanized Parliament and the public, but so did arguments about how to manage and maintain the slave trade. As historian Abigail Swingen observes, "it became commonplace for all sides to portray the enslavement of Africans as essential to the economic functioning of the empire, which had emerged to buttress and sustain white mastery."[19] Even abolitionists argued for a partial or piecemeal

---

17. Home Office, *UK Action Plan*, 4.

18. See Logan Rae Gomez's "Temporal Containment and the Singularity of Anti-Blackness" and Stuart Hall's "Racism and Reaction" on historical amnesia.

19. Swingen, *Competing Visions of Empire*, 9.

end to slavery in order to protect British interests. The *Action Plan* historiography decontextualizes the diverse arguments for abolition and underpins a white savior complex wherein freeing slaves becomes a British enterprise and accomplishment. It celebrates Britishness as agentic and abolitionist while decentering the anti-Blackness and racism informing Britain's extensive history of slave trading and postcolonial immigration restrictions.[20]

Portraying its link to slavery as severed, the UK also aims to settle accounts with another coin connected with slavery. In a *Guardian* editorial, Lola Young, a Black member of the House of Lords, comments that governments "exhibit squeamishness whenever the linked questions of apologies and compensation are raised."[21] Young quotes the secretary of the Equiano Society, Arthur Torrington, who points out that the British government offered an apology in the 1830s to *enslavers*, not to enslaved people, and paid £20 million in reparations for the property lost when the enslaved were freed. As scholar of English Marcus Wood trenchantly notes, "Britain's societal response to 2007 hid behind a date, and used 1807 as a monolith, (or is it a shibboleth?), to avoid thinking of the outfall of the slave trade now."[22] Historian David Olusoga situates this type of amnesia:

> Few acts of collective forgetting have been as thorough and as successful as the erasing of slavery from Britain's "island story." If it was geography that made this great forgetting possible, what completed the disappearing act was our collective fixation with the one redemptive chapter in the whole story.[23]

Abolition is that redemptive chapter. While that chapter has been officially closed in relation to reparations for the descendants of slaves, the *Action Plan* strategically reopens it to advance an antitrafficking agenda in the lauded tradition of British abolitionism.

Britain's struggle with the legacies of slavery and questions of accountability is visible in Labour Prime Minister Tony Blair's public statement in 2006 on the British Empire's role in the transatlantic slave trade. No previous British prime minister had ever condemned the slave trade so directly, which in itself is saying something. Blair stated,

> Personally I believe the bicentenary offers us a chance not just to say how profoundly shameful the slave trade was—how we condemn its existence

---

20. Kempadoo, "Modern-Day White (Wo)Man's Burden."
21. Young, "Truth in Chains."
22. Wood, "Significant Silence," 163.
23. Olusoga, "History of British Slave Ownership."

utterly and praise those who fought for its abolition, but also to express our deep sorrow that it ever happened, that it ever could have happened and to rejoice at the different and better times we live in today.[24]

Using the words "shameful" and "sorrow," Blair condemned the existence of the slave trade and praised abolitionists but also took the opportunity to link the bicentenary to modern-day slavery. "We also need, while reflecting on the past," Blair continued, "to acknowledge the unspeakable cruelty that persists in the form of modern[-]day slavery."[25] But Britain was there to help, since, Blair assured, "We also need to respond to the problems of Africa and the challenges facing the African and Caribbean diaspora today."[26] Casting Britain's response not as paying reparations but as figuring out "how we can help Africa tackle its problems," Blair's text bore the hallmark of a neoabolitionist approach by claiming to bestow freedom on others through antitrafficking efforts in the UK and bilateral aid abroad, while Britons "rejoice at the different and better times we live in today."[27]

The invocation of a transhistoric abolitionism allows Blair to encode his commemorative statement with historical amnesia. Put another way, the most robust rhetoric from a British prime minister against the violence of the transatlantic slave trade turned into the veneration of British abolitionism and, moreover, Britishness. Catherine Hall, chair of the Centre for the Study of the Legacies of British Slave-Ownership (now called Centre for the Study of the Legacies of British Slavery), writes that Blair "expressed his *regrets* that something bad had happened, but stopped short of the apology (which would have indicated responsibility and notions of restitution) that he had been pressed to make."[28] Blair's passive sorrow that the slave trade "ever happened," as Hall argues, aimed "to sidestep the question of reparations," but it was "symbolic too of a wider reluctance to confront an awkward history."[29] Historical amnesia was a response to calls for the British state to apologize for the slave trade, particularly during its celebration of abolition.

According to historian Douglas Hamilton, the separation "between slavery and abolition in the British imagination is longstanding."[30] For instance,

---

24. Blair, Slavery: "Bicentenary of the Abolition."
25. Blair, Slavery: "Bicentenary of the Abolition."
26. Blair, Slavery: "Bicentenary of the Abolition."
27. Blair, Slavery: "Bicentenary of the Abolition."
28. Hall, "Britain 2007," 197.
29. Hall, "Britain 2007," 197. After negative press and reaction to his statement on slavery, Blair uttered the word "sorry" in 2007 to apologize for Britain's role in the slave trade.
30. Hamilton, "Representing Slavery in British Museums," 132.

Hamilton recounts the circulation of a commemorative painting in 1808 that portrays Britannia, the symbol of Britain in female form, "bathed in sunlight while the chains of slavery lie broken at her feet."[31] The *Action Plan* claims 1807 in a similar fashion, disavowing legacies of an imperial project that enslaved millions and redrew the world map. It denies British slavery's endurance after that date by decontextualizing the history of abolition to pitch a contemporary criminological project. But, unlike the Britannia painting, the *Action Plan* uses 1807 to stretch abolition transhistorically into the future. Abolition is appropriated and presented as an appropriate event for framing the UK antitrafficking agenda. Trafficking rhetoric visualizes the relationship of Britain to slavery through broken chains, while casting as credible the links it draws between African enslavement and European migration.

By representing slavery strategically to depict Britain as antithetical to it, the *Action Plan* creates a history, and a cartography, wherein slavery comes from elsewhere and enters the UK. It locates East Europe in particular as an origin point of trafficking, and Britain in turn becomes the endpoint at which such violence gets checked. The UK government soft-soaps its plan to combat unwanted immigration, representing itself as an abolitionist nation, not as heir to an empire built on slave labor and a neoliberal state engaging in racialized border control. Framed as a solution to trafficking, the *Action Plan* insists that border control serves the interests of people exploited in, but not by, Britain. The UK thus asserts its national sovereignty via border control, which is warranted by modern-day slavery rhetoric that demands Britain defend itself and helpless others from foreign practices of unfreedom.

The next section offers alternative historical referents for the *Action Plan* to challenge the linking of transatlantic slavery with trafficking and abolition with the UK antitrafficking agenda. First, I complicate claims that Britain severed its connection to slavery in 1807, by giving a fuller history of anti-slavery legislation, including its criminalization in Britain—for the first time—in 2009. Second, I offer another historical anchor for the *Action Plan* to show how the nineteenth-century panic over white slavery is a better link to the border logics at work in the UK's modern-day response to immigration.

BORDER LOGICS OF WHITE SLAVERY AND SUPREMACY

The Slave Trade Act of 1807 outlawed the transport of people into slavery, but not slavery itself. People previously transported or born enslaved remained in

---

31. Hamilton, "Representing Slavery in British Museums," 132.

bondage until passage of the Slavery Abolition Act of 1833, which nominally freed slaves within the British Empire while permitting slavery to continue in Saint Helena, Ceylon (Sri Lanka), and East India Company territories. The Slavery Abolition Act paid compensation to 46,000 slave owners, which was "the largest bailout in British history until the bailout of the banks in 2009."[32] Slaves received no compensation but were instead forced to continue providing unpaid labor for their former masters, as most British colonies instituted a so-called apprentice system after abolition, compelling manumitted people to work in "slave-like" conditions. "In effect," Olusoga explains, "the enslaved paid part of the bill for their own manumission."[33] References to abolition obscure this protracted process and erase the role of the enslaved and formerly enslaved in fighting slavery. In the *Action Plan,* the UK venerates abolition while eliding how slavery ended within and outside of Britain. The UK's strategic use of history distracts from two facts: Britain practiced and profited from slavery after 1807, and it did not outlaw slavery inside its borders until 2009.

At the time of the bicentenary, no law categorically prohibited slavery inside of Britain. That criminal offense—holding a person in slavery or servitude, or requiring them to perform forced or compulsory labor—appeared in Section 71 of the Coroners and Justice Act and passed with little fanfare in 2009. To explain the two-century delay in prohibiting slavery in Britain, the UK government framed Section 71 not as a recognition of endogenous practices of slavery but as a response to slavery's sudden arrival. The absence of domestic legislation served to support the convenient narrative that slavery existed outside of Britain. Criminalizing slavery in the twenty-first century was therefore not an abolitionist triumph but a newly necessary legal intervention. In this way, Section 71 confirmed the antitrafficking agenda's claim that the UK was defending itself from slavery.

Although slavery was seen as an external problem, fears about an internal slave trade in white women have a historical precedent in Britain. The white slavery panic took hold several decades after the Slavery Abolition Act 1833, when the British Empire was grappling with its still-shifting relationship to its former slaves. "The very name 'white slavery' is racist," argues sex work scholar Jo Doezema, "implying as it does that slavery of white women was of a

---

32. Olusoga, "History of British Slave Ownership."

33. Olusoga, "History of British Slave Ownership." Olusoga recounts that it was enslaved people and taxpayers who paid the £20 million that the Slavery Abolition Act put aside to compensate enslavers, which amounted to 40 percent of the total government expenditure in 1834. Colonists argued that the apprentice system was necessary to teach slaves how to be free before their full emancipation.

different, and worse, sort than 'black' slavery."[34] Imperial angst propelled fears about a traffic in white women while minimizing the enduring impacts of slavery on Black people. White slavery rhetoric shifted focus from the brutal realities and legacies of transatlantic slavery to the illusory threat of enslavement of white English women by nonwhite foreign men. This moral panic was "a global phenomenon, or, more precisely, an *imperial* one."[35] As historian Judith Walkowitz details in her classic work on Victorian prostitution, the moral panic over white slavery "had all the symptoms of a cultural paranoia overtaking Britain," which found its industrial supremacy threatened by the United States, its global empire threatened by Germany, and its class system threatened from within.[36]

Initially, "white slavery" referred to labor exploitation under industrial capitalism, but it came to mean the sexual exploitation of white women and girls. London physician and antivice advocate Michael Ryan popularized this second meaning in his book, *Philosophy of Marriage in Its Social, Moral and Physical Relations,* published in 1837. In its pages, Ryan railed against an "infernal traffic" that he declared was "carried on to a great extent, principally by Jews."[37] As he described it, "white-slave dealers trepan young girls into their dens of iniquity, sell them to vile debauchees, dress them out in fine clothes, and take from them all the wages of their horrible calling."[38] In the twenty-first century, antitrafficking advocates claim to fight sexual exploitation and human rights abuses but, in the nineteenth century, antivice advocates, who were frequently also racial purity activists, proclaimed a fight against prostitution and miscegenation.[39] For Ryan, miscegenation threatened marriage, a sacred institution that the state and white society arranged as an *intra*racial exchange in women.

The racist story of Jews ruining white womanhood cemented the template for future sex slave panics that depicted foreigners capturing white women and girls and compelling them to sexually service men of diverse races. In the Victorian era, white slavery stories turned on the alleged darkness of slave traders and the men purchasing sex. White women who had sexual relations with nonwhite men were seen as defiled or depraved, that is, these women were either rape victims or race traitors. Racialized rape tales portrayed white

---

34. Doezema, "Loose Women or Lost Women?," 30.
35. Devereux, "'Maiden Tribute,'" 1.
36. Walkowitz, *Prostitution and Victorian Society,* 247.
37. Ryan, *Philosophy of Marriage,* 14.
38. Ryan, *Philosophy of Marriage,* 14.
39. See Doezema, *Sex Slaves and Discourse Masters*; and O'Connell Davidson, *Modern Slavery.*

prostitutes as helpless victims in order to make sense of interracial sex. Anti-vice advocates impugned men for prostitution and miscegenation, but prostitutes were likewise tarnished by disreputable sexual and racial contact. Strictly speaking, white slaves were not fallen women who were viewed as willfully engaging in vice, but still they had little chance of returning to the social standard of white womanhood due to their sexual experience.

Also stoking the white slavery panic was the fear that white women might choose to have sexual relations with nonwhite men. Then as now, white women posed a sexual danger to nation-states predicated on white supremacy, because white women possessed the power to effect racial downfall. White women's reproductive capacity to create something other than a white populace made them a manifest threat to white dominance. Antivice agendas thus employed the symbolic white slave and her condemnable cousin, the willing prostitute, to combat women's independent, and independence, movements.[40] Historians of the white slavery panic argue that cultural shifts and colonialism, which induced white women's proximity to nonwhite men, caused fears about migration and sexual accessibility.[41] In keeping with the goal to control white women, antivice agendas curtailed their migration to cities and to other countries via policy and public awareness campaigns. Antivice agendas pitched mobility restrictions as safety measures to protect women from sexual slavery. The stated intention was to protect sexual purity, but preventing migration blocked white women's access to economic and sexual opportunities, which were sometimes the same things.

State antivice commissions never uncovered an organized traffic in white women, and prostitutes rarely received recognition or protection as "white slaves." Because most prostitutes could not meet the social standard of racial and sexual purity to count as white slaves, they did not get state protection but rather faced the intensive policing that shaped crusades to save white slaves. Yet the panic about white slavery grew into a transatlantic movement, enthralling Britain and the United States, which codified the White Slave Traffic Acts and launched campaigns to suppress prostitution, miscegenation, and immigration. Regarding US white slavery ideology, historian Frederick Grittner argues, "white slavery represents the power of a metaphor to reduce the complex problem of prostitution to a simple story of villain and victim, while at the same time arousing public awareness and increasing pressure for a solution."[42] *Transatlantic white slavery* was a metaphor that shifted racialized

---

40. Doezema, "Loose Women or Lost Women?," 21.

41. For historical accounts of the white slavery panic, see, for example, Bristow, *Prostitution and Prejudice*; Grittner, *White Slavery*; and Donovan, *White Slavery Crusades*.

42. Grittner, *White Slavery*, 133.

representations of slaves from Black to white, to keep white women away from other races and delink white people from the evils and legacies of *trans-atlantic slavery.*

VISUALIZING TRAFFICKING VICTIMS

Moral panic theory is helpful for mapping how the *Action Plan* frames migratory trends through a good-versus-evil story. In this case, the moral panic's object—human trafficking—is depicted as an evil and organized crime that threatens women's safety and national security. But moral panic theorists have argued that a panic's object—be it drugs, mugging, music, or witchcraft—does not in fact pose a dire threat, and they instead locate the causes of panic in cultural and economic shifts within a society.[43] The sudden and unprecedented arrival of East Europeans after the 2004 EU expansion triggered fears about losing jobs, culture, and even the English language. In the wake of EU expansion and economic competition, additional fears about immigration and crime coalesced into panic over a traffic in East European women. The UK government made it harder to migrate legally, including for East EU citizens who had the right to move in the EU and the UK. A key text in the agenda, the *Action Plan* defined modern-day slavery in order to delimit the discursive field as part of its plan of attack. Paraphrasing Braidotti, policing access to full EU citizenship results in a racialized hierarchy, construing East Europeans as peripherally white and as secondary to the European core and British whiteness.[44] Its racialized formula is a function of othering in response to EU expansion.

In the previous sex panic, white slavery narratives were cautionary tales about what could happen to white women and white society. Trafficking rhetoric likewise works as a warning. The figure of the trafficking victim foreshadows what could befall not only migrant white women but Britons too. In trafficking imagery, victims are visualized as white East Europeans who can also be (read as) white Britons. The visual rhetoric constructing the trafficking victim thus contradicts hegemonic whiteness, which is assumed to have mastery over itself and others, in contrast to the abject slave who lacks autonomy. Discursively linking East Europeans to slavery distances them from British value(s). Trafficking rhetoric warns that migration can end in East Europeans

---

43. For theories of moral panic, see Cohen, *Folk Devils and Moral Panics*; Young, *Drugtakers*; Goode and Ben-Yahuda, *Moral Panics*; and Hall et al., *Policing the Crisis.*

44. Braidotti, "On Becoming Europeans," 34.

being tagged and turned into commodities, while the UK is reduced to a place where slavery happens.

Inside the *Action Plan,* a full-page public awareness poster visualizes trafficking victims. The poster shows a window with three people arranged inside it, their backs against a brick wall. Framed by windowpanes, a white woman, man, and girl wear price tags with the words "Human Trafficking" written below a barcode. In the final frame, a close-up of the price tag describes the commodified people: "Item: Human Being, Model: Male/Female, Size: S/M/L, Price: Priceless." They are also labeled with what look like passport stamps, which read "Labour Exploitation," "Sexual Exploitation," "Modern Slavery," et cetera. Questions at the poster's center address its imagined audience: "Did you arrange your own travel to the UK? Do you know who you are meeting in the UK? Do you know where your journey is leading in the UK?" In 2007, trafficking rhetoric presupposed an audience of East Europeans, as suggested by the visual representation of white people only. Of course, an argument could be made that whiteness is not meant to indicate a particular group, that is, the poster represents racelessness. Whiteness, then, represents Human Being, a white supremacist trope couched as universal appeal. While race is held constant in this representation, the poster expands the focus beyond *sex trafficking* by including a man and child as well as stamps labeled "Labour Trafficking" and "Trafficking in Children." In this way, the whole nuclear family is at risk of trafficking, reminding all migrants to stay in their home countries or end up in an even more forbidding place.

Written in English, the poster also addresses a British audience. The textual and visual juxtapositions, including a list of sponsoring organizations' logos below the windowpane, imply that trafficking targets migrants, but it threatens Britons too. Britons are at risk of subordination to EU immigration and the serious organized crime it cloaks. The poster instructs Britons how to see other white people and suggests that traffickers are those who arrange travel or offer to help migrants upon arrival in the UK. The myopic focus on individuals relies on the "assumption that their choices produce the problem. The conditions of formal and informal labor dissolve into the background."[45] Indeed, the poster spotlights individuals, leaving the structural factors that shape migration as opaque as a brick wall. It places structural factors outside of the frame by intimating that trafficking results from victim gullibility and criminal greed. The framing of East Europeans as victims or as "21st century traffickers" turns victimhood and criminality into individual traits, as opposed to contingent legal statuses ascribed by the state. Spotlighting white migrants

---

45. Suchland, *Economies of Violence,* 73.

allows the UK government to deny that it engages in racial profiling and racist immigration policy. The poster directs the gaze to white trafficking victims blinded by a light in their eyes, while viewers are instructed to "OPEN YOUR EYES!" Still, the state's structuring presence is visible because the lower border of the poster is a lineup of national, international, and NGO agencies including the UK Home Office, UN International Organization for Migration, and Crimestoppers tip line.

Painting East Europeans as liabilities (albeit priceless ones) advances the accusation that the UK gives, rather than gains, due to immigration. While migrants provide the UK with cheap and crucial labor, trafficking rhetoric frames the exchange as British hospitality to, and potential harm from, foreigners. The state appeals to British viewers to see migrants through a trafficking lens by soliciting Britons to participate in border logics and a border project. This project aims to produce border controls across the UK, materialized as divisions between Britons and others who ought to face suspicion and oversight. National borders are not simply the edge of state territory; borders are also made by marginalizing others and telling citizens to see migrants as suspect.

ANTITRAFFICKING AS BORDER PROJECT TO PROTECT BRITISH VALUE(S)

Like the earlier panic about an internal slave trade, Britain's management of borders to secure its status, and to ensure only certain people can lay claim to it, also has a historical precedent. In this section, I concentrate on the Nationality Act of 1981, which redefined British citizenship as a genealogical property belonging to white people. The 1981 Act stripped former colonial subjects of British citizenship and residency rights and restricted their immigration. Whereas the British Empire "took in" people to rule them, Thatcher's government contested postcolonial subjects' claims to British nationality. Codifying that nonwhite people from the former colonies did not belong *in* Britain, because they no longer belonged *to* Britain, the 1981 Act declared that only people with proof of descent from an ancestor born in the British Isles could reside or hold citizenship in Britain. The legal stratagem aimed to (re)produce a white nation, predicated on racial superiority, by bonding past, present, and future generations. It meant Australians with a British ancestor could become nationals through this route, but Barbadian descendants of slaves could not. It constructed a legal pathway for white people in Commonwealth countries, while introducing immigration barriers and diminished legal standing for nonwhites. According to sociologist Imogen Tyler, it illustrates "the manufacturing of a fear by and among the ruling elites that Britain was losing its sense of national identity as it lost its hold on the empire."[46] Likewise, the 2016 Brexit referendum exposed "the manufacturing of a fear by and among the ruling elites" that the UK was losing its national identity and sovereignty due to the EU and changes in its geopolitical standing. Since the empire's demise, Britain has no longer defined itself through colonial dominance and expansion. Rather, the UK has redefined itself through immigration control and extraterritorial projects to align other states with British interests.

Governments across the UK political spectrum explained immigration policy by referring to an imperiled British identity in need of legal support and protection. Indeed, Tyler explicates that the "associative link established in the 1981 Act between post-imperial national identity, democratic freedom and immigration controls has since been cemented into a form of common sense within British government policies."[47] The *Action Plan* further cements this associative link. In 2008, Prime Minister Gordon Brown announced New Labour's new immigration stance in the speech "Managed Migration and Earned Citizenship." In it, Brown lays out the danger of losing sight of the UK's destiny. Allow me to quote at length:

> Indeed there is a real danger that while other countries gain from having a clear definition of their destiny in a fast changing global economy, we may lose out if we prove slow to express and live up to the British values that can move us to act together. So the surest foundation upon which we can advance socially, culturally and economically in this century is to be far more explicit about the ties—indeed the shared values—that make us more than a collection of people but a country. This is not jingoism, but practical, rational and purposeful—and therefore, I would argue, an essentially British form of patriotism.[48]

Brown's speech justified the UK's U-turn on permitting East EU citizens open access to its labor market. The Labour government folded its defense of Britishness into a closed-door immigration policy. In this pivotal speech, Brown expresses a fear that Britain loses from immigration while others gain from it. His government must prioritize British values to protect the nation's future. Brown defends this "essentially British form of patriotism" and its evaluation of migrants in this way:

---

46. Tyler, *Revolting Subjects*, 58.
47. Tyler, *Revolting Subjects*, 58.
48. Brown, "Managed Migration and Earned Citizenship," 1.

And by being more explicit about what it means to be a British citizen we can not only manage immigration in a way that is good for Britain—for our citizens, our way of life, our society, and our economy—but at the same time move forward as a more confident Britain—a Britain living up to shared values, a Britain equipped to lead economically, a Britain able to succeed as a 21st century society, enriched by change but anchored in enduring ideals.[49]

Through the rhetorical device of anaphora, Brown reiterates the possessive pronoun "our" and the proper noun "Britain" to voice an anxious desire that Britishness belongs to a certain people and retains a certain value. It should be enriched but also anchored. Immigration policy to secure that value, and to ensure it is not lost or cheapened, requires that the state define who is valuable enough to belong in Britain. Value for Britain, under the earned citizenship scheme, is produced through a five-tier points-based system that labels and commodifies people. Brown says that Tier 1 is for "the most highly skilled, designed to attract the brightest and the best to Britain," while Tier 3 exists "in case there is a need for low-skilled labour—but we are currently not letting anyone into Britain through this route."[50] Constructing such a "community of value," as Bridget Anderson calls it,[51] means that only top-tier people are "seen as constituting the worthwhile part of the national imaginary, as opposed to the 'shirkers' or 'scroungers.'"[52] The state applies value to migrants, and citizens, through sorting processes tethered to immigration policy and discourse. Hence, the people in a community of value "are not just of value to the nation, as productive and respectable individuals," Forkert and coauthors argue, "they are also the figures whose lives are treated, in policy and in public discourse, as of the most value, as worthy of consideration and care."[53] By representing trafficking as a problem of migrants enslaving each other, the *Action Plan* masks how the state creates value and risk when determining who can migrate, live, and work legally.

The prime minister's speech indexes efforts to keep the UK distinctive—not European, but British—by managing migration and citizenship as a member state in an expanding EU. If Britishness is tied to a valuable identity, then the arrival of tens of thousands of migrants can be presented and perceived as threatening the historical bonds between country and citizen. But the project to render the UK as a country constituted by distinctly valuable people fails,

---

49. Brown, "Managed Migration and Earned Citizenship," 9.
50. Brown, "Managed Migration and Earned Citizenship," 5.
51. Anderson, *Us and Them?*, 2.
52. Forkert, Jackson, and Jones, "Whose Feelings Count?," 180.
53. Forkert, Jackson, and Jones, "Whose Feelings Count?," 180.

because, to produce itself, Britain has been and remains tied to and dependent on other people and places. Brown admits this dependence, with a curious claim to British exceptionalism, when he asserts, "the idea of citizenship can be addressed more cogently here in Britain than elsewhere because for centuries Britain has been made up of many nations."[54] Putting this spin on empire, Brown explains, "As the first—and probably the most successful—multi-national state in the world, we have always had to find ways of bringing people into a United Kingdom."[55] The inclusivity he views as distinctly British was predicated on imperialism and colonialism as "ways of bringing people" into Britain "for centuries." Seeing no contradiction here, the prime minister venerates Britain's inclusive history in a speech announcing immigration restrictions.

In this context of growing fear about EU migration, as well as UK membership in the EU, trafficking rhetoric mediated both physical and symbolic borders, often depicting white migrants as threats, or as threatened, while telling Britons to act against the people putting their country at risk. In the sixteenth century, the British Crown unleashed a border project to expand its empire across the globe. In the twenty-first century, the UK government implemented a border project to curtail immigration. Rhetorically, the UK promotes this project by using analogies of slavery and abolition to rewrite history and build support for its antitrafficking agenda. Framing the *Action Plan* as descending from an abolitionist past, the UK government can talk about slavery while it installs nationalist policy that commodifies and devalues people. In this way, trafficking rhetoric constrains history and immigration to manage *and* manufacture fear about Britain's past, present, and future.

CONCLUSION

A 2019 United Nations report on racism and intolerance advises that the UK government "still has not adopted a country-wide strategy or action plan that addresses racial discrimination and inequality in a comprehensive fashion."[56] The lack of anti-racist action plan is significant given the speed at which the government created an antitrafficking action plan for a crime defined as new. Acting with an urgency not seen in response to racial discrimination and violence, the UK made a plan to recognize an exceptional category of modern-day slaves but refused to recognize the material legacies of transatlantic

---

54. Brown, "Managed Migration and Earned Citizenship," 1.
55. Brown, "Managed Migration and Earned Citizenship," 1.
56. United Nations Human Rights Council, *Report of the Special Rapporteur*, 5.

slavery for descendants of enslaved Africans. Constructing the exceptional victim, antitrafficking policy mediates fears about the weakened links between race and national identity. This category of victim is separated from economic migrants, asylum seekers, and refugees, who are seen as willfully entering the UK. Partitioning people in this way recalls the moral division made between white slaves and willing prostitutes.

The white slavery panic offered an outlet for racial anxiety by depicting white women as threatened, casting nonwhite men as sexual and thus existential threats. The persuasive conceit of whiteness taken and ruined expressed fear for the nation's future and sought to preserve its racial order. The UK antitrafficking agenda updates this ideology by configuring unwanted migrants as threatening to ruin Britain. The rhetorical resonances between the white slavery and modern-day slavery narratives indicate that slavery *had* been imagined as internal to Britain before. However, then as now, this imaginary can only tell stories of racialized threats to Anglo ethnic whiteness.

Whereas the white slavery panic policed imperial borders, the trafficking panic polices national borders to protect an attachment to cultural purity. Purity—whether framed as a matter of race or culture—imagines Britishness as a certain, and superior, kind of whiteness. Desires to protect and purify the British Empire and the British state both turn on deep-rooted racial logics.

UK trafficking rhetoric associates East Europeans with crime while celebrating Britain for abolishing the slave trade. Human trafficking is defined as a serious threat requiring action against migrants to protect the country and women from exploitation. This agenda subordinates East Europeans through immigration restrictions and moral stories that frame them as a problem. Since there are numerous white ethnic groups in East Europe, tying them to modern-day slavery accomplishes the rhetorical legerdemain of displacing Blacks as the focus of slavery's afterlives by centering whites as slavery's real victims. Trafficking rhetoric exploits an event from the past to forget Britain's slaving history and claim that the UK can save other whites from enslavement. The use of 1807, a date in a larger history that warrants reflection, does not cite the precedent for the antitrafficking agenda so much as cloak state violence against migrants and minority citizens.

CHAPTER 3

Glaring Whiteness

Trafficking Visual Rhetoric and Tropes of Blindness

An antitrafficking poster displays a geographical outline of the United Kingdom filled in with a collage of houses and buildings that epitomize rural,
suburban, and urban regions. Outside of the visual images depicting British
landscapes, black space surrounds the UK, situating it as a target destination
for human trafficking. The map does not show the whole picture, however,
or present accurate geography. To emphasize the national borders of the UK
only, emptiness fills the space where the Republic of Ireland ought to be, rendering that country and former colony invisible.[1]

On top of this background, black print highlighted in bright blue declares,
"Women and children are being trafficked in the UK and forced into the
sex industry." Underneath this claim, small white print warns, "It could be
in your town. Or your street. In your community. In your workplace. Don't
close your eyes. Look around you." Repeating the possessive pronoun "your"
underscores that the town, street, community, and workplace all belong to the
poster's intended audience: British citizens.[2] Human trafficking, by contrast, is

---

1. The Republic of Ireland participated in the antitrafficking operation Pentameter 2,
making its absence from the map notable. Although UK trafficking rhetoric depicted a transnational traffic in white women, Irish women were not depicted as victims in this discourse.

2. Chapter 2 discusses Prime Minister Gordon Brown's use of the possessive pronoun
"our" in a speech on migration, underscoring who belonged in the UK and to whom the UK
belonged.

construed to be an exogenic crime that is happening in the UK, to elicit feelings of shock and anger at the outrageous offense of sex slavery. "It" comes from elsewhere and enters "your" town, street, community, or workplace. In this context, "your workplace" strikes an odd note, since it is unlikely that the message aims to imply that its audience works in the sex industry. More likely, the aim is to express visually and verbally that trafficking is everywhere. The wording is vague, but the poster conveys a sense of urgency about trafficking's sudden arrival.

As part of the Blue Blindfold campaign by the UK Human Trafficking Centre (UKHTC), the poster makes a public appeal akin to anti-terrorism campaigns, stating: "If you see something, call Crimestoppers." The something that British citizens might see is not specified or visualized, because the UK's trafficking narrative had already framed East European "women and children" as the victims "forced into the sex industry." As Pardis Mahdavi and Christine Sargent point out, however,

> human trafficking does not just affect "women and children." It is a phenomenon undeniably rooted in gender inequalities, but to limit the experience of trafficking to members of only one gender or cohort is both inaccurate and unethical. Yet, this phrase "women and children" consistently dominates the issue, to the point where the continuous repetition of the phrase has turned it into "womenandchildren," which can easily collapse into "women as children."[3]

The campaign's command to call the Crimestoppers tip line reassures British citizens that they can remain anonymous when identifying others to authorities. Not only "women and children" but also *foreign* men who fit the discursive profile of *trafficker* should be watched by concerned citizens. Regarding neighborhood watch programs, Sara Ahmed has argued that "the subject who watches out for crime, is also *maintaining the value of her or his neighbourhood*."[4] Indebted to Ahmed's insight, I claim that in Blue Blindfold's visual economy, the citizen who watches out for crime is also maintaining the value of their nation. That value is secured through a national surveillance project, something akin to a *nationhood* watch.

Blue Blindfold instructs its British audience to defend the nation by watching others and making anonymous tips about them to the state. It devolves

---

3. Mahdavi and Sargent, "Questioning the Discursive Construction," 15–16.
4. Ahmed, *Strange Encounters*, 27.

authority for detecting trafficking to the average Briton, who acts as a surrogate for the law and immigration enforcement apparatus.[5] Surveillance is individuated, because every citizen should look out for signs of trafficking. At the same time, taking an aerial view, Blue Blindfold aspires to assemble the collective gaze of citizens by putting antitrafficking eyes everywhere. Recalling the speculative figures in chapter 1, the researchers who created the first UK estimate of trafficked women described their task as "looking for needles in haystacks."[6] That metaphor resonates with Blue Blindfold's exhortation because citizens must observe countless migrants to find the few that the state will rescue. Given the campaign to locate trafficked women and children, I offer a brief overview of the institutional landscapes that migrants, refugees, asylum seekers, and victims of trafficking had to navigate.

In 2007, after the conclusion of the antitrafficking police mission, Operation Pentameter, the Labour government established the UK Human Trafficking Centre to develop intelligence on trafficking, raise awareness, and coordinate police operations (including Pentameter 2, discussed in chapter 4). The UK hailed the UKHTC as the first of its kind in Europe, positioning itself as a world leader in antitrafficking efforts. According to the Home Affairs Committee, the UKHTC's goal was to forge "closer links between the immigration service and law enforcement" because transnational crime created the need to enmesh immigration and law enforcement even further.[7] Starting in 2009, the UKHTC and the UK Border Agency (UKBA) co-ran the National Referral Mechanism (NRM) that assessed claimants applying to the state for victim of trafficking status. The UKHTC processed the people from the UK and European Economic Area, while the UKBA handled those from outside of these regions.[8] The UKHTC's name made it sound like an agency offering support to trafficking victims, but it was always housed in law enforcement. First it was housed within the South Yorkshire Police, then the Serious Organised Crime Agency and, later, the National Crime Agency to "bring even greater focus to [antitrafficking] work, putting its full weight behind representing the

5. See Oliviero's "Sensation Nation and the Minutemen" for analysis of surrogates of the nation who act as border patrol.
6. Kelly and Regan, Stopping Traffic, 6.
7. House of Commons, Trade in Human Beings.
8. The Council of Europe Convention on Action against Trafficking in Human Beings required all frontline agencies (e.g., embassies, hospitals, police stations) to train staff to identify trafficking victims. The UK government circumvented this requirement by appointing only two agencies as "competent authorities," the UK Human Trafficking Centre and the UK Border Agency.

UK's interests internationally."[9] The UKHTC's relocations chart its institution-
alization in crime agencies of increasing prominence. The rise of this antitrafficking infrastructure was matched only by its organizational volatility, which
was a feature, not a bug, of the UK's immigration system.

Like the UKHTC, other immigration and law enforcement agencies experienced volatile organizational arrangements. In 2007 the Labour government
set up the Border and Immigration Agency, only to merge it with UK Visas
and HM Revenue and Customs in 2008 to form the UK Border Agency. The
UKBA became one of the largest law enforcement agencies in the UK, but it
lacked coordination and received an avalanche of complaints. The criticism
was so serious that the Parliamentary Ombudsman lambasted the UKBA for
lost applications, a case backlog in the hundreds of thousands, and erratic
treatment of asylum and residence applicants. A report by the Home Affairs
Select Committee deemed the UKBA operationally incompetent. Home Secretary Theresa May abolished the UKBA in 2013, returning executive authority to the Home Office and creating three separate agencies: UK Visas and
Immigration, Immigration Enforcement, and the menacingly named Border
Force. In a mere five years, the state oversight of people entering the UK had
flipflopped from two agencies to one to three, with authority devolved from
the Home Office, only to be restored again. The Labour government touted
its rational policymaking and evidence-based governance, but many people
were forced to navigate a volatile legal terrain with chronic backlogs, changing rules, and inexplicable decisions. Multiple agencies undergoing legal status
changes themselves were deciding who counted as a migrant, refugee, asylum
seeker, or trafficking victim. Organizational volatility lays bare how individual and institutional statuses are contingent, co-constitutive, and tied to state
mandates.

Notwithstanding the infrastructural tumult, 2007 was a banner year for
the antitrafficking agenda. That year alone witnessed the launches of Pentameter 2 (the largest antitrafficking police operation in UK history), the Human
Trafficking Centre, and the *UK Action Plan* on trafficking. It was also the year
of the Blue Blindfold awareness campaign launch. Tightening the conceptual
linking of trafficking and transatlantic slavery, Blue Blindfold's messaging circulated during the bicentennial celebration of Britain's abolition of the slave
trade. As chapter 2 covers, the UK yoked the years 1807 and 2007 to analogize
human trafficking with transatlantic slavery and antitrafficking efforts with
abolition. Although the UK government used modern-day slavery rhetoric,
thereby relying on transatlantic slavery tropes, trafficking was depicted as

9. Home Office, *Human Trafficking*, 12.

happening to foreign white women. Trafficking rhetoric circa 2007 never centered Black and brown people as victims. Bicentenary hype venerated Britain for stopping people trafficking while Blue Blindfold veiled the state violence entailed in law and immigration enforcement.

In what follows, I hope to elucidate how the Blue Blindfold campaign twists blindness to promote nationwide surveillance. The campaign lodges trafficking in the mind's eye to produce British citizens as neoabolitionists who think they are participating in a national effort to stop a crime constructed as anathema to British values. To do so, it makes trafficking mean something significant to Britons by framing it not as some far-flung problem, but as something they might stumble upon in their town, street, community, or workplace. In this way, Blue Blindfold scripts surveillance into everyday life. While the campaign asks little of Britons beyond watching others and picking up the phone, it imparts a weighty moral responsibility because foreign women and children's fates lie in British hands. This neocolonial scenario chimes with Mary Louise Pratt's notion of "the seeing man," whom she defined as "the white male subject of European landscape discourse—he whose imperial eyes passively look out and possess."[10] But in a significant twist, Blue Blindfold relies heavily on the white female subject to convey its message. She appears on awareness posters as the white British woman who is blind to trafficking, but who could see it if she would just open her eyes! Yet there is a figure of white womanhood that does not appear on posters. The archetypal trafficking victim's absence requires viewers to fill in the hidden premise of this visual argument.

OPEN YOUR EYES AND SEE FOR THE STATE: BLUE BLINDFOLD'S VISUAL RHETORIC

Rhetoric scholar J. Anthony Blair maintains that "visual arguments are typically enthymemes—arguments with gaps left to be filled by the audience."[11] An enthymeme is a syllogism to which an audience supplies the absent or hidden premise. By not explicitly announcing its premise, the awareness campaign Blue Blindfold depends on shared knowledge and unspoken assumptions to communicate its enthymematic message. A common cultural background enables the audience to read and decode meaning embedded in

---

10. Pratt, *Imperial Eyes*, 9. Pratt's description of the seeing man calls to mind the statue of Edward Colston discussed in the book's introduction. The statue's gaze is at once passive and possessive.

11. Blair, "Rhetoric of Visual Arguments," 52.

the communication. Wendy S. Hesford explains, "Images may be more immediate and memorable than words at the sensory level but, like all texts, images
acquire social value and symbolic overtones from larger frames of reference."[12]
The frames of reference allowing Blue Blindfold to express its message include
the stories about criminal gangs forcing East European women into prostitution. Contextualizing Blue Blindfold for viewers, the stories say who should be
seen, enabling the awareness campaign to work without visualizing or speci-
fying anyone. Without representing victims or perpetrators, the ekphrastic
campaign urges viewers to picture scenes of sexual subjection. Britons are
encouraged to imagine trafficking for themselves while seeking to find it in
real life. Signs of the crime lie in the eye of the beholder.

That is not to say that Britons can interpret trafficking however they
want. Blue Blindfold steers viewers' interpretation of trafficking with visuals
anchored by context and caption. Since only "women and children" and "the
sex industry" are mentioned on the map poster, trafficking is connected to sexual exploitation. No specific mention is made of other victims or of industries
like agriculture, construction, and hospitality. The interplay of text and image
influences public feelings and beliefs about trafficking and viewers' relationship to its occurrence. As scholars of visual rhetoric Helmers and Hill explain,
"We learn who we are as private individuals and public citizens by seeing
ourselves reflected in images."[13] Therefore, British viewers are represented as
"blind" to suggest that saving trafficked women and children requires watchful
citizens. The pedagogical value of awareness campaigns also denotes that "we
learn who we can become by transporting ourselves into images."[14]

The speculative estimates and the antitrafficking proposals analyzed in
chapters 1 and 2, respectively, addressed professional audiences, but evocative
visual materials like Blue Blindfold address lay audiences more than experts.
During the campaign's launch, a Conservative minister of Parliament said,
"Congratulations to the UKHTC on their splendid initiative which will create greater awareness of modern-day slavery using contemporary and eye-
catching advertising."[15] The reference to advertising accurately captures how
Blue Blindfold marketed the antitrafficking agenda to the British public.
Indeed, it was an advertising, marketing, and communications firm that made
"the Blue Blindfold brand and the 'Don't Close Your Eyes' campaign for the

---

12. Hesford, *Spectacular Rhetorics*, 8.
13. Helmers and Hill, *Defining Visual Rhetorics*, 1.
14. Helmers and Hill, *Defining Visual Rhetorics*, 1.
15. BBC News, "Anti-Trafficking Drive Launched."

UKHTC to create awareness of the problem of human trafficking."[16] A marketing firm created the UK's most prominent antitrafficking awareness campaign, but its evocative visuals could be misread as an insult to Britons or as a distasteful portrayal of blindfolded trafficking victims. To clarify its meaning, the UKHTC's head Nick Kinsella stated, "The blindfold represents how people are blind to the fact that human trafficking is not remote, but something that is local and impacts on local communities. It does not represent the victims of human trafficking."[17] The blindfold trope signifies a metaphorical impairment to the moral vision required to see trafficking. Analogizing blindness with ignorance, Blue Blindfold depicts Britons as oblivious but softens this accusation by implying that trafficking blindsided Britain. Trafficking came out of the blue, as it were, and caught the country unprepared for the sudden arrival of modern-day slavery. Kinsella explained further, the "blindfold is a symbol of our ignorance and the need to keep our eyes open to what is going on around us. If people see something, we want them to take positive action by reporting the matter to the local police or Crimestoppers, and not closing their eyes to it."[18] Tapping into visions of national security, Blue Blindfold cultivates a sense (sight) and sensation (suspicion) by binding migration and crime, such that one cannot be seen without the other.

The campaign posters represent the British public as ignorant about trafficking—hence, the need for an awareness campaign—but also as knowledgeable enough to detect trafficking on sight. The posters provide no information about trafficking beyond asserting that it is happening in the UK. This direct but vague assertion cues the visual enthymeme, that is, how the audience already knows what to look for based on shared knowledge. The audience must be familiar with the dominant trafficking narrative to understand the campaign's hidden premise. Blue Blindfold and its audience co-construct that which goes unsaid, and unseen, in the campaign imagery. The British public should watch others for signs of trafficking; the search is for people who look like they do not belong. The visual enthymeme directs the British audience to fill in what is absent or hidden by linking people to a crime discursively tied to migration and enslavement. Trafficking is constructed as something

---

16. Principles Agency, May 6, 2009, https://www.flickr.com/photos/principles/3506355611/. On a later version of the website, Principles Agency described its company mission this way: "We're passionate about beautiful ads, we have after all been making them for 30 years. But we don't ever create beauty without the brains. We know that effective marketing has to do much more than raise eyebrows and turn heads. It's results that we're after—effective, measurable results. That's why everything we do stems from hardworking strategy and creative insight. It's these principles that we live by, work by and put behind our name."

17. National Archives, "Blue Blindfold."

18. National Archives, "Blue Blindfold."

no civilized nation can tolerate and therefore as opposed to British values. This agenda promotes the criminal profiling of migrants and minority citizens of the UK whose appearance is seen as not British, meaning, in material terms, not white. How does Blue Blindfold constitute an audience of white British citizens who view themselves as participating in a national security campaign? How does the campaign's hidden premise authorize unstated but blatant xenophobia and racism? When the blindfold trope travels, how does the enthymeme change but also remain the same? For example, "blindfold Brexit," which was not an awareness campaign but a pejorative phrase naming the possibility of the UK exiting the EU, also used the blindfold trope to express British ignorance toward a grave national threat. This chapter analyzes how Blue Blindfold, and later the idea of blindfold Brexit, used the blindfold trope to express the UK's risky geopolitical position while demanding very different cures for British "blindness." In the first case, Blue Blindfold advocated for restored sight, that is, a certain way of looking to see and save trafficked women and children (and, hence, the British way of life itself) by expelling slavery from the UK. In the second case, blindfold Brexit discourse criticized Vote Leave's false campaign promise to restore sovereignty (and, hence, the British way of life itself) by saving the UK from the EU.

WOMEN ON THE ANTITRAFFICKING FRONT LINES: COLOR, BLINDNESS, AND BRITAIN

Blue Blindfold posters relied heavily on images of white women, featuring them more often than anyone else. The visual rhetorical role of white women communicated the campaign's message of vigilance, vulnerability, and gender violence. In the subsequent sections, I examine the visual rhetoric comprising three Blue Blindfold posters, each one depicting a white woman alone doing an everyday activity. The women are supposed to look like ordinary British citizens. Their attire is nondescript, and they appear middle-aged, not young like trafficked women are assumed to be. The poster women are rendered unremarkable, except for the blue blindfolds over their eyes that mark them as unseeing subjects.[19] A naturalistic appearance shapes the persuasive appeal of the images by underscoring what does not belong—blindfolds, trafficking—in the "natural" British environment.

---

19. Finnegan, "Naturalistic Enthymeme and Visual Argument." Barring the blue blindfolds, the women appear naturalistic, going about their daily lives and seemingly caught unawares by the camera, which makes them innocent vis-à-vis trafficking.

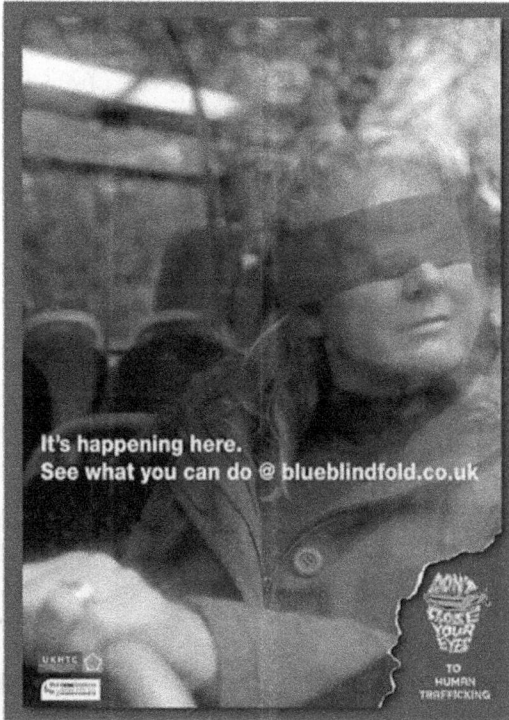

FIGURE 5. Blue Blindfold antitrafficking poster.

The first poster features a white woman standing on a balcony with a clothing line behind her, on which children's clothes are hung to dry. She rests her hands on the balcony and grasps a small garment; there are no children visible. Her expression looks fretful, and she is unsmiling. The second poster shows a white woman riding on a city bus (see figure 5). Her left hand grips the seat in front of her, and she wears a wedding ring. Her face is turned toward the bus window and her expression is serious. A third poster features a white woman sitting on a park bench with a newspaper in both hands. Unlike the other women, her face is in profile, but she also appears to be serious and unsmiling.

Color schemes convey the mood and rhetorical tone of a visual text, influencing viewers' perceptions and interpretation of images. The representational style of Blue Blindfold is somber with muted colors except for a few bright red and blue spots accentuating the sponsor logos and the blindfolds. Red carries a connotation of warning and, on these posters, it draws the eye to the UK Human Trafficking Centre and Crimestoppers logos. Blue connotes a multitude of moods, ranging from optimism to sorrow. Significantly, a secondary metaphorical meaning for *blue* is to talk about or to show sexual acts in an offensive way (e.g., blue humor).[20] Quite apart from other antitrafficking awareness campaigns, Blue Blindfold tries not to be that kind of blue.[21] It avoids sexual imagery altogether, using instead the bright blue blindfolds to grab the public's attention. The ubiquity of sexualized images representing trafficking victims makes their absence in Blue Blindfold rather remarkable. Opting not to visualize victims of trafficking, the campaign renders them as everywhere and nowhere, omnipresent yet invisible. Without trafficking victims to look at, the focal points of the campaign are the white poster women who are styled as maternal (not sexual) objects through the use of visual signifiers such as children's clothes, wedding ring, and newspaper. The poster women are not to be viewed as trafficking victims or sex workers, because they are married, have kids, or read newspapers. Unwittingly, this visual rhetoric reveals how the campaign relies on and reifies stereotypes about women working in prostitution, who supposedly do not have spouses, kids, or reading habits.

While Blue Blindfold does not use sexualized images of women, it relies on gender tropes to define human trafficking and visualize how the state wants the problem handled. First, the campaign assumes trafficking victims are women and children, which, as noted in reference to the conflation of "women and children," has the effect of infantilizing women and feminizing the children viewed as victims. Second, the British citizen who should see trafficking victims is represented as a white woman. As symbol of the nation-state, the white woman has historically embodied anxieties about immigration, racial purity, national identity, and reproductive futures. She is the guardian of citizenship, and we witness that role reprised for her in Blue Blindfold posters, but she is also vulnerable, as is the nation she stands for. Third, men are absent from the scene. Men are nowhere acknowledged as victims of trafficking in the sex industry or any other industry. Evidently, posters cannot envision, or encourage audiences to imagine, women saving men from exploitation. But also, why are men not expected to see trafficking in the sex industry? Since men buy sexual services, wouldn't they need awareness due to their potential proximity to trafficking victims? This fact would raise the issue of British men

---

20. In the United States, blue is associated with police, as evidenced in "the thin blue line" and "Blue Lives Matter." The association of blue with police is less pronounced in the UK. But the London Metropolitan Police, founded in 1829 and heralded as the first modern police force, had dark blue uniforms that inspired police attire worldwide.

21. On victim representation in antitrafficking campaigns, see Doezema, "Loose Women or Lost Women?"; Andrijasevic, "Beautiful Dead Bodies"; and Sharma, "Travel Agency."

hiring sex workers, which Blue Blindfold does not address. Instead, the campaign centers white British women, leaving to the imagination the people who may be more closely entangled in trafficking.

The posters have an ominous atmosphere, and the tagline "It's happening here" warns of human trafficking's proximity. As such, the poster women are "already under threat by imagined others whose proximity becomes a crime against person as well as place."[22] Blue Blindfold tells its audience to look for trafficking, but the campaign visually represents only blindfolded Britons and a map of the UK. That imagery depicts citizens and their country as the bodies threatened by trafficking. The presentation of white British women as the posters' focal point in effect centers *them* as the injured party, blinded and in danger. Traffickers are not only hurting foreign women and children; they are also harming the UK and its people. Britons need to open their eyes because trafficking hits so close to home. And the posters say what to do: "See what you can do @blueblindfold.co.uk." That public appeal aligns British vision (see) and action (do) with the state's point of view. The directive is to look outward, not within. It goes without saying that human trafficking does not belong in Britain, or anywhere near white British women.

The posters simultaneously depict the defective citizen, who cannot see trafficking, and the ideal citizen, who could see it, if they choose to. Thus, the normative citizen has vision, but this gaze is coded as raceless. Blue Blindfold is demanding a certain way of looking to defend a certain way of life.

Despite the different UK backdrops, the poster women are all posed as if they are gazing into the distance. As if, without the blindfolds over their eyes, the women could observe what is happening around them. Notably, each woman is shown alone with no one around to impede her actions. The blindfold disables her, making her oblivious and unable to see or help anyone. But if she casts off the blindfold, then she will be able to do something when she detects the trafficked women and children in front of her. These blindfolded but otherwise unencumbered white British women figuratively clash with trafficked women and children, who are defined as controlled by others and unable to act on their own. The poster women can move from their passive positions to become active participants in the antitrafficking agenda. In this visual schema, white British women are on the front lines in the fight against trafficking. They serve as synecdoche, seeing for the state and being its eyes on the ground. To recast Pratt's incisive concept of "the seeing man," I am arguing that Blue Blindfold posters call for "the seeing woman"—the white female subject whose neoabolitionist eyes scan the nation in search of

---

22. Ahmed, "Affective Economies," 118.

signs of trafficking. In this way, images of white British women express the moral imperative of looking, which Blue Blindfold constructs as a *raceless gaze*. However, in the next section, I explore how the campaign addresses a white British audience by presenting a particular face to signal who looks and who is the object of the gaze.

GLARING WHITENESS IN A GAZELESS FACE

Via the transmogrification of moral blindness into physical blindness, Blue Blindfold portrays British citizens as unable to see trafficking. Disability thus becomes a prop and plot device for the dramatic action of removing the blindfold and restoring sight. The ableist logic subtending this plot device suggests that blindness must be fixed to defend the nation against a foreign foe and save innocent women and children.[23] Britons are urged to see themselves in the campaign's imagery by identifying with the poster women, but also to reject their "unappealing" portrayal as blind to trafficking. Rejecting blindness, however, entails viewers accepting the campaign's main claim that trafficked women and children are concealed in their towns, streets, communities, and workplaces. Blindness is immoral in relation to the (hidden) human trafficking crisis, and Britons are morally obligated to become seeing subjects. But who, exactly, needs to see? And who needs to be seen?

Returning to Kinsella's point about the blindfold as symbol of ignorance, Blue Blindfold claims to fix this incapacity by raising awareness and restoring the moral vision Britons need to see trafficking. Hence, the way to fix British blindness is to proliferate eyes throughout the UK. Michel Foucault described panoptic power as "*a faceless gaze* that transformed the whole social body into a field of perception: thousands of eyes posted everywhere, mobile attentions ever on the alert, a long, hierarchized network."[24] He theorized that this faceless gaze induced a constant feeling of exposure in the people subjected to it, who never knew whether or not they were being watched. Significantly, Blue Blindfold imagery depicts the opposite of what Foucault described. Posters depict a gazeless face—the blindfolded Briton—to show what the state actually wants: *a faceless gaze*, which is everywhere yet attributable to no one. Posters assure Britons that they can look without being seen and call Crimestoppers without their identities being known. In contrast to a gazeless face, which is depicted as both unappealing and immoral, *a faceless gaze* gives

---

23. Kafer, *Feminist Queer Crip*, 3. Kafer contends that disability is constructed as that which must be cast off and left behind in order to secure the future.

24. Foucault, *Discipline and Punish*, 214. My emphasis.

the nation-state an appearance of morality and ability: Britons are opening their eyes to trafficking! With this insidious twist on blindness, Blue Blindfold conjures up the panoptic dream of "eyes posted everywhere, mobile attentions ever on the alert, a long, hierarchized network." The state empowers police and immigration officers to fight trafficking, but citizens are also incorporated into a nationhood watch to transform "the whole social body into a field of perception." As with anti-terror campaigns, antitrafficking is state business that obliges citizens to act as relay points and notify authorities about what alarms them. In some sense, the call is made to all citizens, but Blue Blindfold uses a particular face to constitute its audience and communicate its message.

Posters show white women, who Kinsella made clear do not represent trafficking victims but rather Britons in blindfolds to symbolize their ignorance of trafficking. Yet Blue Blindfold's audience knew who to look for, since it already knew the UK trafficking narrative, the key to the campaign's visual enthymeme. Decoding the hidden premise requires filling in Blue Blindfold's blanks. Who is its target audience? Who does it want its audience to target? Analyzing structural racism alongside claims of colorblindness in Europe, Fatima El-Tayeb argues,

> the continued inability or rather unwillingness to confront, let alone over-come, *the glaring whiteness* underlying Europe's self-image has rather drastic consequences for migrants and minority communities routinely ignored, marginalized, and defined as a threat to the very Europe they are a part of, their presence usually only acknowledged as a sign of crisis and forgotten again in the ongoing construction of a new European identity.[25]

In a similar vein, Blue Blindfold indexes the glaring whiteness underlying Britain's self-image, specifically in the repeated casting of white women in the representative role of British citizen. Blue Blindfold tries to be a colorblind campaign by hiding the rhetorical-material significance of whiteness. In its visual economy, the poster women's whiteness is not to be seen as significant or, for that matter, suspicious. The women represent the ordinary citizen, the national norm, the everyday ethnos. "As the contemporary discourse of color-blindness has taken hold," Lyndsey P. Beutin notes, "scholars have continued to theorize the ways in which seeing—and not seeing—race remain constitutive of power."[26] Put another way, observing the (dis)appearance of race is crucial for grasping how power materializes and comes to matter. In the case

25. El-Tayeb, *European Others*, xxv. My emphasis.
26. Beutin, "Racialization," 12.

of Blue Blindfold, the (dis)appearance of race in antitrafficking representations justifies the state's deployment of panoptic power over people viewed as not belonging in Britain since they are tied to migration and slavery, which marks out migrants and minorities for surveillance. Not to see that Blue Blindfold's use of whiteness is saying something misses its unstated but blatant xenophobia and racist prejudice. Its premise is in plain sight but tries to conceal itself.

One of racism's conceits is that images and stories featuring white people are universal propositions. Assuming whiteness is the normative state of human being excludes other people from the synecdochic role of standing in for everyone. This assumption of whiteness hides the particularity of what is being said and shown, as Blue Blindfold reveals upon closer inspection. By contrast, the decentering and denaturalization of whiteness inserts "an intellectual crowbar between whiteness as 'looking white,' and whiteness as the performance of culture and the enactment of power."[27] Making whiteness stand out by marking its (dis)appearance, "strips a normative privileged identity of its cloak of invisibility," and brings the constitutive work of culture and power into view.[28]

UK trafficking rhetoric defines not only a transnational crime but also a national culture. While the focus seems to be on trafficked women and children, the rhetoric recites a story about Britain's relation to slavery, in the past and present. In part by rescripting a history when Britain traded in human beings, trafficking rhetoric recasts the past through a myopic focus on abolition. This revised history continues to place Britain in hierarchical relation to others. Whether Britain is trading slaves or freeing them, it is discussed as the driver of history, a domineering discourse predicated on ideas of racial and cultural supremacy. Blue Blindfold reflects and reinforces this discourse by juxtaposing Britons, assumed to be white and represented as such, with trafficking victims, assumed at the time to be from East Europe, but not visually represented. In opposition to British whiteness, East European whiteness is made meaningful as a sign of crisis. Trafficked women and children function here as foils to freedom-granting Britons. Blue Blindfold implores Britons not to be bystanders to crime but to be on standby for the state, ready and willing to act. British whiteness is made to appear generous as it generates hostility toward people who are not *that* white, who are helpless, and who are seen as helping themselves to what does not belong to them. Feminist scholars have repeatedly exposed Western states' habit of justifying their military and humanitarian agendas by claiming to rescue non-Western women, thus exhibiting the West's moral and cultural superiority.[29]

---

27. Garner, *Whiteness*, 6.
28. Garner, *Whiteness*, 5.
29. Mohanty, "Under Western Eyes."

Mobilizing the allegorical association of sight with knowledge, the campaign's pseudo-Biblical assertion is that Britons only need to lose their blindfolds and they will see. But what will they see? Will they see women and children "chained to a bed in a brothel"?[30] Since UK trafficking rhetoric referred to forms of sexual subjection that few people will ever witness, Blue Blindfold pointed to what was in plain sight: the unprecedented presence of tens of thousands of economic migrants from East Europe after EU expansion. Of course, wealthy people migrate for work too, but they are classed as desirable arrivals and rarely even referred to as "migrants." The people welcomed to cross national borders are "'nomads,' backpackers, transnational corporate executives, 'expats,' or international and humanitarian workers, who are predominantly white and western."[31] They cross borders with ease when they travel south and east. But when people from the Global South and East travel to the West and North, exclusionary border regimes greet their migration. The UK government determines who can work, reside, and naturalize, not only based on socioeconomic class but also racial and ethnic classifications. As chapter 2 mentions, Thatcher's government passed immigration law to codify Britishness as a genealogical property belonging to white people. But white nationalism tracks to long before Thatcher, taking root in the empire when "England's eighteenth-century domination of the slave trade carried with it the beginnings of the mass diffusion of the modern concept of racism."[32] Arun Kundnani considers the *longue durée* of racism's entanglements with national sovereignty. He writes,

> the end of the British Empire provided the conditions for a reincarnation of racism, as it was reborn in the form of a white cultural nationalism. Those who had been made into colonial subjects as Britain expanded its imperial rule over multiple "races" were now to be excluded from the white nationality that Britain sought in a context of contracting sovereignty.[33]

Anxiety about national sovereignty is fertile ground for reincarnating racism and xenophobia as Britain manages the contradiction of its self-image as an imperial nation, and later white nation-state, over and against its dependence on others to define and sustain itself.

The next section turns to the Vote Leave campaign, which capitalized on anxieties about national sovereignty in the context of the 2016 European Union membership referendum. Vote Leave's slogan, "Take Back Control,"

---

30. Haynes, "(Not) Found Chained to a Bed in a Brothel."
31. Kempadoo and Shih, "Rethinking the Field," 2.
32. Kundnani, *End of Tolerance*, 11.
33. Kundnani, *End of Tolerance*, 15.

aptly captured the complaint that the EU had stolen UK sovereignty on issues like borders, immigration, and international trade.[34] Indeed, from the start, the "campaign gathered around the idea that Brexit was the only way for Westminster to recover its confiscated sovereignty."[35] Sovereignty claims anchored arguments that the UK must escape the EU to control its own destiny without interference from Europe. Given British imperialism and colonialism, the irony of Vote Leave's sovereignty claims was clearly lost on its proponents from across political parties. The UK foreign policy of extraterritorial governance exposes how deeply its double standard of sovereignty runs.

BLINDFOLD BREXIT: BRITISH SOVEREIGNTY AGAINST EU ENSLAVEMENT

The blindfold as a symbol of British ignorance, and potential risks to Britons, reappeared in the debate over Brexit a decade after Blue Blindfold's 2007 launch. The phrase "blindfold Brexit" named the possibility of the UK leaving the EU without a deal detailing the terms of their new relationship.[36] The Brexit referendum received a large voter turnout, with the result tipping at 51.9 percent in favor of Leave.[37] The close result revealed divisions in the UK. England and Wales had majorities for Leave, but Northern Ireland voted to remain in the EU, and Scotland supported the Remain campaign by an overwhelming majority.[38] Moreover, the Brexit outcome bolstered calls for Scottish independence (from the UK, not from the EU). There were divisions within England and Wales as well, particularly with more demographically homogenous areas favoring Leave.[39] Further, "the Irish border was completely forgotten about during the 2016 referendum campaign only to come back with a vengeance during the Brexit negotiations with the EU."[40] Forgetting Ireland recalls its dis-

---

34. Serhan, "In a Bid to 'Take Back Control.'" While the Leave campaign had a very catchy slogan, the Remain side struggled to articulate a clear message stating why the UK should stay in the EU.

35. Ringeisen-Biardeaud, "'Let's Take Back Control,'" 2.

36. For news items on the issue, see, for example, Dixon, "Just Say No"; and Blomfield, "Government's Silence."

37. BBC News, "UK Votes to LEAVE."

38. England showed the highest support for Leave at 53.4 percent, Wales at 52.5 percent, Northern Ireland at 44.2 percent, and Scotland at 38 percent. Majorities in every council in Scotland voted for Remain, revealing the diversity of opinion on the referendum in relation to region.

39. Sternberg, "Europe's 'Nationalism.'"

40. Agnew, "Taking Back Control?," 267.

appearance on the Blue Blindfold poster depicting the UK in an empty black sea. But that imaginary of an isolated UK grates against the historical and geographical reality of its entanglements with other sovereign states, including neighboring nations and former colonies with which it negotiates borders, tax and trade agreements, and Brexit, among many other things.

To begin the two-year negotiation period to leave the EU, the UK had to trigger Article 50 of the Treaty on European Union. Theresa May, the former home secretary who succeeded Cameron as prime minister, triggered Article 50 on March 29, 2017, setting the departure date for that day in 2019. Hence, the UK embarked on an unprecedented process. Pledging to avoid a blindfold Brexit, May requested multiple deadline extensions to negotiate a deal that Parliament and the EU would accept. After failing three times to pass a deal in Parliament, May resigned, and Boris Johnson, whose platform was "Get Brexit Done," replaced her. "It was clear," Perrigo writes, "those three words had helped win Boris Johnson's party an overwhelming majority," the largest since Thatcher.[41] A prominent figure in the Vote Leave campaign, Johnson was dead set on exiting the EU, but he also wanted to avoid a blindfold Brexit. After four years of political turmoil, the UK finally struck a deal with the EU and exited in 2020, thereby ending almost half a century of EU membership and becoming the only state to leave the bloc.

To explain the Vote Leave campaign's shock victory, Virdee and McGeever contend that "two contradictory but inter-locking visions" contour UK politics and culture.[42] The first vision, they write, "comprises an imperial longing to restore Great Britain's place in the world as *primus inter pares* that occludes any coming to terms with the corrosive legacies of colonial conquest and racist subjugation."[43] The second vision, by contrast, imagines the UK stepping away from the global stage and returning to "little island" status. The visions are contradictory yet share a common desire for an illusory past. One desires the past expanse of influence (Global Britain) while the other sees a future in national insularity (Little England). They animate what are, in effect, complementary impulses to extend UK interests globally while exiting the EU to manage borders and immigration. All of that would supposedly come with the restoration of sovereignty. According to international relations specialist Robin Niblett,

> The idea of restoring sovereignty appeals to British sensibilities. It speaks to the independent spirit of a small island on the edge of Europe. It speaks to

41. Perrigo, "Get Brexit Done."
42. Virdee and McGeever, "Racism, Crisis, Brexit," 1802.
43. Virdee and McGeever, "Racism, Crisis, Brexit," 1802.

British voters' pride in their history, their democracy, their ability to govern themselves (and in days gone by, much of the world) without interference from foreign powers.[44]

But Brexit's pledge to restore sovereignty offered not only a false promise but also a false choice, since absolute sovereignty is a partisan fairy tale. Political geographer John Agnew explains,

> the logic behind the drive for Brexit has been part of a normative political project on the part of UKIP [the UK Independence Party] and the right-wing of the Conservative Party: to make sovereignty and territory match has always been the goal of such nationalist movements. Once in power, of course, many of them have found it difficult not to find rationales for expanding both their territorial and overall spatial scope at the expense of others. This is how English nationalism produced Britain and the British Empire.[45]

Yet Brexit campaigners insisted that the EU dominated the UK, thus forcing the UK to free itself from EU entanglement and take control back from Brussels, the de facto EU capital. Brexit's two "contradictory but inter-locking visions" of expansive empire and insular island not only further entrench but also amplify racism and xenophobia. As a United Nations report warned, "national debates and certain practices and policies before, during and after the Brexit referendum in 2016 have amplified racial discrimination, xenophobia and related intolerance," which political parties across the spectrum egged on and exploited.[46] "What often gets elided in discussions of Brexit," Virdee and McGeever observe, "is the presence of what we might term 'internal others' against whom the nation has often defined itself, including, most notably, racialized minorities and migrants."[47] Expanding this point, Amy Clarke writes,

> the exclusionary effects of Britishness' racial connotations are evident in the blanket labelling of Black, Asian, and Muslim people as migrants, hyphenation of British-Asian and Black-British identities, persistence of colonial discourses, marginalisation of "off-white" migrants, and routine misrecognition of British people of colour as non- or not really British.[48]

44. Niblett, "Sovereignty Argument."
45. Agnew, "Taking Back Control?," 260.
46. United Nations Human Rights Council, *Report of the Special Rapporteur,* 17.
47. Virdee and McGeever, "Racism, Crisis, Brexit," 1803.
48. Clarke, "Recognising British Bodies," 2.

UKIP built its political brand on racist and xenophobic rhetoric, but the Labour Party also struck an anti-immigration tone and tapped into intolerance when its political fortunes dwindled. In the 2008 local elections, Labour faced its worst outcome in forty years. It also finished in third place, behind the Conservative Party and UKIP, for the UK section of European Parliament. Following these dismal results, Gordon Brown resigned as prime minister, and Labour tried to "consolidate an anti-migrant working class vote" by aligning with Blue Labour, a group advocating conservative views on crime, immigration, sexual minority rights, and EU membership.[49] To recapture white working-class votes, Blue Labour claimed to place "family, faith and work at the heart of a new politics."[50] At Blue Labour's 2009 public launch, its figurehead, Maurice Glasman, explained the feeling behind the name (Labour was no longer "New" but "Blue"): "It's also 'blue' because it's a sad moment—in a Miles Davis kind of way."[51] The sadness was over the Labour Party's loss of white working-class voters, presented as the central victims of globalization and immigration. Blue Labour pitched a Manichean struggle between white Britons and racialized migrants and minorities, for resources as well as the heart and soul of Britain. No version of the Labour Party, blue or otherwise, captured the 2010 general election, despite the courting of white nationalist sentiment. By forming a coalition government, the Conservatives and the Liberal Democrats ended sixteen years of Labour leadership. David Cameron led the coalition until a majority Conservative government was elected in 2015. Prime Minister Cameron's victory speech reiterated his pledge to hold a national referendum on EU membership. To court Eurosceptics in his party, Cameron had made that pledge two years earlier when he campaigned for Conservatives to win the next general election. Cameron's compromise set Brexit in motion, even though he did not expect a Leave campaign to succeed. He resigned as prime minister, also as promised, after the Brexit vote tipped in favor of the UK leaving the EU.

CONCLUSION: LITTLE ENGLAND OR GLOBAL BRITAIN?

The chapter opened by describing an antitrafficking poster of a map of the UK, floating alone in empty blackness. Returning to this image, we may now see that it perfectly captures the vision of an insular island. Indeed, the Blue Blindfold campaign expresses the two visions—expansive empire and insular

---

49. Virdee and McGeever, "Racism, Crisis, Brexit," 1813.
50. Stratton, "Labour."
51. Stratton, "Labour."

island—outlined by Virdee and McGeever. But where is the vision of expansion? Is a rendition of Global Britain visible anywhere in these state-sponsored antitrafficking materials?

Looking closely at the Blue Blindfold posters, one can see a small icon resembling a globe on the lower right-hand corner (see figure 5). The corner of the posters featuring white British women looks like it was ripped off to reveal a hidden world. The globe icon is hidden under the primary image of the women engaged in quotidian activities. Locating the globe under the primary image hints that trafficking is hidden beneath the surface of normal, everyday life. In contrast, on the poster depicting the map, the globe is on top of the UK. Its location suggests that trafficking is imposed on the UK and that undesirable global elements could overtake the country. Both insinuations intend to sow fear but also fidelity in fighting trafficking for British audiences.

Beyond its strategic locations, the visual rendering of the globe icon itself is significant. It resembles not only a globe but also a human head made of letters spelling out the phrase "Don't Close Your Eyes." A blue blindfold separates the words "Don't" and "Close." And "To Human Trafficking" is arranged to resemble a neck and shoulders holding up the head. The blindfolded head, or globe, is literally filled with trafficking rhetoric. The visual proposition conveyed by this image is that the world and the people in it are blind to trafficking. Given that dire circumstance, the UK is helping British citizens and people around the world to see trafficking and build their capacity to tackle it. Sociologists Kempadoo and Shih contend that the "white westernized / global North [trafficking] discourse has circulated globally and is at times mobilized by local actors, thus masking its geo-political epistemic location."[52] Blue Blindfold's trafficking discourse is not exogenous to but a rhetorical invention of the UK, materializing through the state apparatus and circulating globally, its masked imagery crucial to its movement.

Clever visuals facilitated the success and transnational flow of the Blue Blindfold brand. The US State Department's *Trafficking in Persons Report* praised Blue Blindfold for its efforts "to establish an international symbol for human trafficking and promote a unified campaign that reaches across borders."[53] Multiple countries made copycat campaigns. In 2008, the Republic of Ireland launched its own blue blindfold campaign in order "to encourage police authorities, front line professionals and the public to open their eyes to

---

52. Kempadoo and Shih, "Rethinking the Field," 5.
53. US State Department, *Trafficking in Persons Report,* 42.

human trafficking."[54] And, in 2010, Public Safety Canada and Canadian Crime Stoppers rolled out a campaign with images of Canadians in blindfolds.[55] The US Department of Homeland Security likewise created the Blue Campaign; its website explains that the "name references the global anti-human trafficking symbols the Blue Heart and the Blue Blindfold, as well as the 'thin blue line' of law enforcement."[56] Animated by the same surveillant logic as Blue Blindfold, its website includes a drop-down box labeled "SEE. CALL. SAVE." When clicked, the box gives information for the US Immigration and Customs Enforcement (ICE) Homeland Security Investigations' anonymous tip line.

The transnational adoption of the Blue Blindfold brand signals its overall success as an antitrafficking signifier, empty enough for use in different countries and contexts. It is notable, however, that the copycat campaigns took place in former British colonies with majority white populations. Although Ireland, Canada, and the United States differ in significant ways, they also share similarities in fomenting moral panics about immigration and trafficking. Blue Blindfold's transnational influence positions the UK as a major player on the global antitrafficking market. Ultimately, the campaign's circulation reveals how an antitrafficking brand can travel with ease, while raising alarms about human migration.

As a self-proclaimed antitrafficking world leader, the UK deploys its personnel and uses development aid to compel other countries to engage in "capacity-building" projects that benefit Britain. These projects, explains Sharron A. FitzGerald, instruct "sovereign nations to participate in the work of ensuring the integrity of the UK border and immigration control."[57] For example, the Serious Organised Crime Agency (SOCA) assembled a liaison officer network of "more than 110 posts in almost 40 countries."[58] The *UK Action Plan on Tackling Human Trafficking* notes that the liaison officers "collect and report intelligence from overseas sources; plan and execute intervention activ-

---

54. Department of Justice and Equality, *History of the Blue Blindfold Campaign.* Ireland copied Blue Blindfold's antitrafficking message, including the globe image, while enjoying its global branding as the "Celtic Tiger." From the mid-1990s to late 2000s, Ireland became one of the richest countries in West Europe and experienced a drop in emigration and rise in immigration. The 2008 global financial crisis ended its incredible economic growth, but while Ireland (with the UK and Sweden) implemented an open-door policy toward new EU states, it also launched its own Blue Blindfold campaign as concerns grew about trafficking, economic migration, and pressure on public services.

55. Smith, "Feds."

56. US Department of Homeland Security, "About Blue Campaign." The United Nations runs the Blue Heart Campaign to raise awareness globally about trafficking.

57. FitzGerald, "Vulnerable Geographies," 192–93.

58. Home Office, *UK Action Plan,* 45.

ity overseas in support of SOCA's tasked operations; and develop and sustain effective operational and capability overseas by building partnerships with UK and international agencies."[59] The UK justifies this extraterritorial governance by citing threats to its borders and national security. A government report on trafficking affirms, "Our strategy will give a renewed focus on prevention overseas, a stronger border at home, tougher action on the perpetrators and better identification and care for the victims."[60] Additionally, it warns that "there is more to do to stop the problem before it reaches the UK and raise the importance of the issue abroad."[61] The report represents other countries as incapable of tackling trafficking without UK assistance and supervision. In foreign policy discourse, inducing sovereign nations to align themselves with the UK antitrafficking agenda is cast as capacity-building. The UK imposes its interests on others as a way of exercising sovereignty and demonstrating global prominence. The act of giving is, once again, a form of taking, no longer as explicit empire-building but rather rebranded and expressed as the humanitarian building of the capacity of others. The UK asserts sovereignty by pointing to states that it alleges cannot self-govern and thus need British supervision to tackle trafficking. In this way, humanitarian resource-extraction works hand in glove with extraterritorial governance.

In sum, antitrafficking addresses two deep desires at once: the insular island that lifts the drawbridge, and the expansive empire that leads the world and extends its influence over foreign lands. The UK antitrafficking agenda brings the seemingly conflicting desires together, not only holding this contradiction but appearing to satisfy it. The closed-door immigration policy toward East European EU member states works with, not against, UK extraterritorial governance within "source countries." The UK takes back control, freeing itself from enslavement to EU rules and regulations, while imposing its interests on sovereign states. This double standard of sovereignty is evident in the UK building its global brand on the back of other countries, and Brexit breaking up the EU over its supposed theft of British autonomy.

59. Home Office, *UK Action Plan,* 46.
60. Home Office, *Human Trafficking,* 4.
61. Home Office, *Human Trafficking,* 12.

CHAPTER 4

"A Really Hostile Environment
for Illegal Migrants"

State Violence, Misery, and Immobility

In 2012 Home Secretary Theresa May laid out the Conservative Party's goal to make the United Kingdom "a really hostile environment for illegal migrants."[1] Before she uttered those infamous words, the Labour government had already begun in 2007 to construct a hostile environment for unauthorized workers. During that pivotal year in the UK's antitrafficking agenda, the Labour Immigration Minister Liam Byrne announced plans to fine employers who hired people without the right to work. "What we are proposing here will, I think, flush illegal migrants out," Byrne explained. "We are trying to create a much more hostile environment in this country if you are here illegally."[2] The government wanted employers to check each job applicant's immigration status or risk receiving fines up to £10,000 for each unauthorized worker. Before immigration raids on workplaces became routine, employers were incentivized to reduce fines by reporting unauthorized workers, creating punitive links among the state, employers, and workers. In this way, the hostile approach encouraged employers to hire people assumed to be British, which led to discrimination and the racial profiling of job applicants. When the Conservatives beat Labour, their government intensified the hostile environment by no longer requiring proof that employers knowingly hired unauthorized workers,

---

1. Hill, "'Hostile Environment.'"
2. Travis, "Officials Launch Drive."

doubling fines to £20,000 per unauthorized worker, and creating an offense of "illegal working" that allowed the state to confiscate workers' wages as "proceeds of crime."[3]

Prior to the avowed Hostile Environment Policy, successive governments in the UK had injected anti-immigration hostility into administrative policies and laws. Striking a tough stance, Labour Home Secretary John Reid advocated for spectacular enforcement raids "whether or not 'immigration' was an empirical 'problem.'"[4] Outdoing the Labour Party, the Conservative 2010 election manifesto pledged to reduce annual net immigration to the "tens of thousands."[5] Prime Minister May made the pledge again in 2017 despite the Conservatives already missing the target for six years in a row. Evidently, reiterating an utterly unattainable goal to slash immigration was more important than attaining it.

Beyond blocking entry, another way to attack immigration was to force migrants to leave the UK. Hence, the Hostile Environment Policy's strategy of immiseration by obstructing access to vital services to force migrants out of the country and deter others from traveling to the UK. In pursuit of "a really hostile environment," a Parliamentary Hostile Environment Working Group, later renamed the Inter-Ministerial Group on Migrants' Access to Benefits and Public Services, proposed policies to make daily life difficult for irregular migrants and their families.[6] Regarding its human targets and political significance, immigration experts Griffiths and Yeo contend, "the hostile environment heralded a step-change expansion of everyday borders that is unprecedented in the UK in its scale, scope and speed."[7] The UK pursued an avowed policy to make migrants' lives miserable while claiming to practice a rights-based and victim-centered approach to human trafficking.

IMMISERATION AS IMMIGRATION POLICY

The Immigration Acts of 2014 and 2016 codified a raft of restrictions on employment, housing, healthcare, education, and social security benefits. The UK government encouraged employers, landlords, healthcare providers, and

---

3. Webber, "On the Creation," 79.

4. Forkert, Jackson, and Jones, "Whose Feelings Count?," 181.

5. BBC News, "Tories to Keep." The net migration pledge was made in the 2010, 2015, and 2017 Conservative election manifestos.

6. Webber, "On the Creation," 77; Allsopp, Sigona, and Phillimore, "Poverty among Refugees"; and Aitkenhead, "Sarah Teather."

7. Griffiths and Yeo, "UK's Hostile Environment," 522.

school personnel to check the immigration status of people they encountered while performing their professional duties. The Conservative government also piloted a "right to rent" program in 2014. It went nationwide "despite an (unpublished) Home Office survey indicating it was not working and was leading to greater racial discrimination in the housing rental market."[8] Unable to rent accommodation, people can become homeless, an avoidable situation but one that advances the government's goal of creating hostile conditions. Further, the "right to rent" program harmed the very people that the UK claimed to protect. As the United Nations warned, "asylum seekers and victims of trafficking do not have a right to rent and must gain 'permission to rent' from the Home Office, which can further deter landlords from renting to such individuals."[9]

Proving to be as cruel as its name sounded, the Hostile Environment Policy also punished people for being unhoused. State agencies obtained migrants' private information from charities for the homeless in London while immigration enforcement teams searched for migrants without housing, who were then deported. After an investigation into the euphemistically named Rough Sleepers Support Service, *The Observer* published an article revealing that "emails sent by senior Home Office immigration officials show how they used information that was designed to protect rough sleepers to target vulnerable individuals for deportation."[10] Frances Webber, vice-chair of the Institute of Race Relations, argues:

> the Treaty of Rome gives EU nationals rights to move freely around the EU for work, homeless EU nationals from eastern Europe found sleeping rough in London have had their identity documents confiscated, which prevents them from obtaining employment, and they have found themselves detained and deported for "abuse" of free movement rights.[11]

The Rough Sleepers Support Service ended after *The Observer* exposé, but Home Secretary Priti Patel revived it in 2021, offering assurances that consent would be obtained before state agencies accessed migrants' data.[12] Of course, the assumption that consent can be neutrally obtained in a hostile environment disregards how migrants are coerced to cooperate with state agencies.

---

8. Webber, "On the Creation," 78.

9. United Nations, *Report of the Special Rapporteur,* 15.

10. Townsend, "Home Office."

11. Webber, "On the Creation," 80.

12. Townsend and Walawalkar, "Home Office Revives Plan." A common British term for houseless persons is "rough sleepers."

Also, migrants may think that homeless charities operate separately from the state and protect personal data. The Hostile Environment Policy's "explicit intention is thus to weaponize total destitution and rightlessness," writes Webber, "so as to force migrants without the right to be in the country to deport themselves, at low or no cost to the UK."[13]

In addition to employment and housing, the national health system became entangled in immigration control. The Home Office created a memorandum of understanding (MOU) for the National Health Service and Department of Health to share patients' immigration status. Amid public outcry and objections from healthcare providers, the Home Office withdrew the MOU in 2018 but not before scaring migrant and minority communities about the potential hostility they would face if accessing healthcare. The UN Special Rapporteur reported that pregnant migrants avoided giving birth in UK hospitals, as did "women with legal status or entitlement to legal status because many fear that 'hostile environment' immigration policies will nonetheless result in harm to themselves or their loved ones."[14] British minority citizens also avoided healthcare facilities due to fear that they might be mistaken for "illegal migrants" and mistreated. In light of the findings, the UN Special Rapporteur observed, "It is no surprise that a policy that ostensibly seeks to target only irregular immigrants is destroying the lives and livelihoods of racial and ethnic minority communities," and noted that many of those impacted "have been instrumental to the prosperity of the United Kingdom for decades, and are rightful claimants to citizenship."[15] She condemned the Hostile Environment Policy for stoking xenophobia and for further entrenching racism in the UK.

Rightful claimants to citizenship, like sympathetic victims of trafficking, are discursively divided from the "illegal migrant." Rather than reinscribe that unsustainable division, I consider the Hostile Environment Policy as an assertion of UK sovereignty that expands the state's reach into people's lives while curtailing the rights and mobility of targeted populations through legal and administrative processes. Information on antitrafficking police operations is restricted from public view too. The proactive policing and processing of people under antitrafficking and anti-immigration banners expands surveillance and criminalization, curtails rights and mobility, and enacts state violence, while the UK venerates itself as a world leader of a human rights, victim-centered approach to trafficking. I focus on the Pentameter policing operations and the National Referral Mechanism to conclude my longitudinal

---

13. Webber, "On the Creation," 77.
14. United Nations, *Report of the Special Rapporteur,* 9.
15. United Nations, *Report of the Special Rapporteur,* 15.

rhetorical-material analysis, which began with the first UK estimates of trafficking and ends with the infrastructures built into state agencies to tackle
trafficking. I seek to show how the antitrafficking agenda emboldened the UK
government to make some people's lives miserable because it claimed to set
others free.

POLICING HUMAN TRAFFICKING: A SHINING
EXAMPLE AND A GREAT SUCCESS

Beginning in 2005, a multiagency police-led campaign was launched to target
trafficking for sexual exploitation. Its four-month pilot, code-named Operation Pentameter, tested surveillance on the "type of location likely to be used
for exploitation," meaning massage parlors, hotels, and private residences
suspected of facilitating prostitution.[16] The operational overview document
articulated an "opposition to the attitude that prostitution is inevitable," framing the abolition of prostitution as an attainable and desirable goal.[17] It linked
abolition to a civilizing mission when declaring "there is no place for such
practice in our so-called civilised 21st century."[18] In this sentence, the practice
in question is prostitution, not trafficking. This hostile rhetoric matched the
objectives of the Home Office's Coordinated Prostitution Strategy for England
and Wales to:

- challenge the view that street prostitution is here to stay
- achieve an overall reduction in street prostitution
- improve the safety and quality of life of communities affected by prostitution, including those directly involved in street sex markets
- reduce all forms of commercial sexual exploitation.[19]

While the rhetorical emphasis lies on street prostitution, the Labour government was at the time promoting intolerance toward all forms of prostitution.
The Home Office report, *A Coordinated Prostitution Strategy*, used language
that sounded like antitrafficking rhetoric when advocating for intolerance. It

---

16. UK Border Agency, *Enforcement Instructions and Guidance*, 9.6.1. The other phrase
used for suspicious locations was "vice premises," recalling Victorian-era rhetoric from the
white slavery panic. Operation Pentameter's scoping phase surveilled locations and its active
phase, when raids took place, ran from February to May 2006.

17. Gloucestershire Constabulary, *Pentameter Operational Overview*, 2.

18. Gloucestershire Constabulary, *Pentameter Operational Overview*, 2.

19. Home Office, *Coordinated Prostitution Strategy*, 1.

propounds, "Street prostitution is not an activity we can tolerate in our towns and cities. Nor can we tolerate any form of commercial sexual exploitation, whether it takes place on the street, behind the doors of a massage parlour or in a private residence."[20] The state switched tactics, from advocating *tolerance zones* for prostitution to cracking down on street and indoor prostitution, including brothels and walk-ups where the law required that prostitutes work alone. The UK agenda against *sex trafficking* heated up the political climate around prostitution, giving the state a warrant to intensify policing in order to improve "the safety and quality of life of communities affected by prostitution." The agenda facilitated crackdowns on legal and illegal forms of prostitution and immigration, expanding surveillance and the policing of prostitutes and migrants.[21]

Publicizing Pentameter: State Hype and Hyperpolicing

Operation Pentameter's name is a nod toward the poetic. A poem is in pentameter form when a line of verse measures five metrical feet. The pilot Pentameter operation covered the five regions of England, Wales, Scotland, Northern Ireland, and the Channel Islands. Operation Pentameter was heralded as "the first proactive policing operation to simultaneously involve all 55 forces in the United Kingdom."[22] It was a complex multiagency affair. First, the Home Office funded the operation, and Reflex, a task force set up to tackle organized immigration crime, managed it. The National Criminal Intelligence Service and Serious Organised Crime Agency assembled a team to coordinate its daily tasks. Second, it received strategic and tactical help from the Home Office, UK Immigration Services, the Crown Prosecution Service, Crimestoppers, and the Association of Chief Police Officers. Third, representatives from the Poppy Project and Churches Against Sex Trafficking in Europe (CHASTE) were part of Pentameter's gold command group and gave advice on operational strategy. The assemblage of state agencies, NGOs, and charities displayed the UK's seriousness in tackling trafficking. A national antitrafficking police operation was the brainchild of then detective chief superintendent Nick Kinsella. As chapter 3 discussed, Kinsella headed the UK Human Trafficking Centre, a crucial hub in the antitrafficking infrastructure that emerged from Operation Pentameter's purported success. The *Pentameter Operational Overview* publicized its initial results as follows:

20. Home Office, *Coordinated Prostitution Strategy*, 1.
21. Hill, "Demanding Victims," 82.
22. Gloucestershire Constabulary, *Pentameter Operational Overview*, 1.

- 515 Premises visited
- 188 Women rescued
- 84 Women confirmed as trafficked victims
- 232 Persons arrested
- 134 Persons charged to date.[23]

The precise choice of nouns and verbs, and the erasure of the subject, hides who performed the action. The document uses passive constructions to describe proactive policing, euphemistically referring to police raids as "premises visited." As the antitrafficking agenda unleashed state action against people in the sex industry, it also obscured the violence entailed in arrest, detention, deportation, and incarceration. Official rhetoric recoded police raids as rescue operations, while declaring that women detained by the state had been freed from sex slavery. The rhetorical distinction between "Women rescued" and "Women confirmed as trafficked victims" points to the underlying belief that women need to be rescued from trafficking *and* prostitution. Further, a terminological shift conceals who was arrested and charged. The word "Women" disappears and, instead, the gender-neutral "Persons" becomes the operative term. That shift in terms performs two torques at once. It conceals that Operation Pentameter arrested and charged women. And it relies on the fact that the assumption will be that the "Persons" arrested and charged were men. In short, the document revealing the results of Operation Pentameter seeks to hide that the police-led campaign actually contradicted the dominant narrative that trafficking was a crime in which men sexually exploited women. The operation undercut the story of the state saving women from men because it arrested and charged women involved in prostitution. Yet Dr. Tim Brain, gold commander of Operation Pentameter, hailed it as "a shining example of partnership working," demonstrating "what can be achieved when people from a variety of disciplines work together towards a common goal."[24] A lot of official talk hyped Operation Pentameter for surpassing expectations, building momentum, and exposing the tip of the trafficking iceberg.

The operational overview records that the "Pentameter media subgroup harnessed media support and forged valuable links in order to bring the issue to the fore."[25] In addition to media interviews and press releases, Pentameter had a media launch followed by a conference to raise awareness in the travel

23. Gloucestershire Constabulary, *Pentameter Operational Overview*, 1.
24. Gloucestershire Constabulary, *Pentameter Operational Overview*, 2.
25. Gloucestershire Constabulary, *Pentameter Operational Overview*, 3.

industry about human trafficking and antitrafficking efforts.[26] As with the first UK trafficking estimates, the state and media created a discursive circuit in which they cited each other to hype the antitrafficking strategy, which grew from relying on speculative figures to promoting the spectacle of raids and arrests.

Four months after Operation Pentameter, the Home Office launched a larger operation in 2007 code-named Pentameter 2.[27] Alongside the state agencies, NGOs, and charities from the pilot Pentameter, joining this operation were the Republic of Ireland, Northern Ireland Office, Foreign Office, and the UK Border Agency. The expanded enterprise raided 582 private residences, 157 massage parlors, and 83 hotels and ports. A press release from the Association of Chief Police Officers (ACPO) announced that Pentameter 2 rescued 351 trafficking victims. The number later dropped to 167 victims; however, the figure fluctuated depending on the source. For instance, the Gloucestershire Constabulary's annual report said, "As a direct result of Pentameter 2, more than 160 vulnerable people have been saved from lives of abuse, exploitation and misery."[28] While the official numbers dropped, trafficking rhetoric remained hyperbolic. With a number less than half of the original figure of 351 trafficking victims, the police stressed what the operation "saved" the victims *from*—"lives of abuse, exploitation and misery."

Like the victim count, the initial number of suspects also fell, from 528 to 406 suspects. A significant number, 153 people, were "released weeks before police announced the success of the operation," most with no charges at all, while 47 people received police cautions for minor offenses.[29] Most of Pentameter 2's arrests did not lead to trafficking charges. Rather, the big haul from the multiagency police-led operation was 76 people who were convicted for drugs, driving, or prostitution offenses.[30] Overwhelmingly, convictions obtained as a direct result of Pentameter 2 referred to petty crimes, not the serious organized crime of human trafficking. That fact did not stop government officials from touting the capture of trafficking gangs as the successful outcome of the operation. Echoing praise for Pentameter 2, Labour Home

---

26. State antitrafficking agendas ask the media and the travel industry to participate in awareness and police campaigns. This strategy copies anti-terror agendas. See Hill, "How to Stage a Raid"; Ritchie, "Feeling for the State"; Shih, "Fantasy of Spotting Human Trafficking"; and Schwarz and Grizzell, "Trafficking Spectacle."

27. Depending on the document, Pentameter 2 is also written as Pentameter II or Pentameter Two. I use Pentameter 2, except when directly quoting a source that employs an alternative spelling.

28. Gloucestershire Constabulary, *Chief Constable's Annual Report 2008/2009*, 19.

29. Davies, "Inquiry Fails."

30. Davies, "Inquiry Fails."

Secretary Jacqui Smith recycled the trafficking trope of civilized modernity versus savage criminality:

> Pentameter 2 has been a great success. It is an excellent example of partner-ship working[,] and I would commend all those involved who have made a real impact in rescuing victims and bringing to justice those who exploit them. Human trafficking has no place in modern society[,] and I am abso-lutely determined that we continue to take tough action to disrupt these criminal gangs.[31]

Nick Kinsella, speaking as the head of the UKHTC, agreed that "Pentameter 2 has been a great success and now the results need to be analysed in depth, to see what we have actually found."[32] Making the exact same rhetorical move as Dr. Tim Brain, Kinsella claimed success prior to in-depth analysis of an opera-tion. The premature celebrations of Pentameter 2 carried on until journalist Nick Davies published data from an internal UKHTC report, revealing that Pentameter 2's results undercut claims that it was a "shining example" and a "great success." Official claims to that effect had misled the public. In the next section, I parse what the UKHTC report said and how Pentameter 2's results unraveled officials' trafficking rhetoric, revealing the human costs that they, and the hostile environment, hid from public view.

ASSESSING THE STATE: PENTAMETER'S FAILURE COMES INTO PUBLIC VIEW

The UK Human Trafficking Centre's internal report bore a long, cumbersome title. Not drafted for dissemination into the public domain, the report was titled *Statistical Assessment of Victims Recovered and Suspects Arrested dur-ing the Operational Phase of Operation Pentameter Two* (hereafter *Statistical Assessment*). Its contents were restricted from public view. Its cover page listed five handling instructions for anyone who saw it. The instructions advised that the report contained sensitive material and could only circulate in govern-ment departments in accordance with security regulations. Additionally, the instructions stated that the *Statistical Assessment* was "supplied in confidence and may not be disseminated beyond the agreed readership / handling code recipient without prior reference to UKHTC." The instructions reiterated that

---

31. *Independent,* "Trafficking Crackdown Frees 170 Victims."
32. Association of Chief Police Officers in Scotland, "Operation Pentameter 2 Exposes Human Trafficking."

none of its contents could be disclosed. If concern about the *Statistical Assessment* was not already evident, the cover page also advised that the handling instructions should not be detached from the report. Given how much government, police, and UKHTC officials had talked about Pentameter 2, these restrictions indicate a pivot in the state's antitrafficking communication strategy. The report wore an anxious cover because its contents revealed the manifest failure of Pentameter 2.

The *Statistical Assessment* records that Pentameter 2 "recovered" 164 victims, that is, less than half of the number initially broadcast in the press release by the Association of Chief Police Officers.[33] On the contrary, the *Statistical Assessment* notes that police struggled to put people into categories and that "22 individuals have been removed from the suspects total as they were also recorded as victims."[34] In addition to categorizing the same person as a suspect *and* as a victim, the police categorized people in similar situations as suspects *or* as victims, thereby destabilizing the binary opposition constructed between trafficker and trafficked, as well as demonstrating an inability to tell the difference.[35] In chapter 1, I explicated how researchers commissioned by the Home Office used police data as an "accurate base" for estimating trafficked women. Five years after *Stopping Traffic*'s estimate, Pentameter 2 exposed that police data was far from dependable, and no assumptions should be made to call it accurate. On the one hand, researchers extrapolated from earlier estimates of London prostitutes to create speculative figures of trafficked women for the whole UK, thus conflating categories to invent nationwide numbers. On the other hand, the police forces implementing Pentameter 2 struggled to put people into categories, despite the idea that victims were easily identifiable on sight (see chapter 3 on the Blue Blindfold campaign). In fact, police forces were bedeviled when trying to classify who was a trafficker and who had been trafficked. They had trouble determining who was a prostitute and who was a trafficked woman. Was a woman one or the other? Could she be both? This confusion surfaces the critical point that police forces were not only arresting women but that the conflation of prostitutes and trafficking victims in estimates did not appear in practice. This revelation meant that women bore the brunt of Pentameter 2. The anti-prostitution abolitionist ideology that all prostitutes should be viewed as victims did not prevent their criminalization but facilitated it.

The *Statistical Assessment* recorded that 35 of the 164 women categorized as victims had "voluntarily" left the UK and that the UK Border Agency

---

33. UKHTC, *Statistical Assessment*, 8. Fluctuating numbers circulated about how many victims of trafficking Pentameter 2 recovered.

34. UKHTC, *Statistical Assessment*, 10.

35. UKHTC, *Statistical Assessment*, 2.

had "removed" 16 victims due to their immigration status.[36] Additionally, 32 women categorized as victims declined support, while 39 others absconded. State agencies did not know their whereabouts. The immigration status of the victims in ten cases had not been decided, but seven additional cases referred to the UK Border Agency got lost in the system. Officials did not know the whereabouts of those victims either. According to the report, one victim received support from a "partner organization," and eleven others "remain in the UK either with NGOs or other support."[37] The government's mantra about promoting a "victim-centred human rights approach" grates against the reality that the UKHTC's own account reveals that only 12 out of 164 victims (7 percent) received support. In other words, most of the victims identified by Pentameter 2 departed the UK "voluntarily," were deported, or disappeared. But that was only part of the story. Other people who were categorized as victims of trafficking faced criminal charges. The state's avowed role as rescuer and protector of vulnerable people "saved from lives of abuse, exploitation and misery" seems speculative at best.

The *Statistical Assessment* recorded 27 victims of trafficking charged with criminal and immigration offenses. In addition, victims were given police cautions for prostitution, controlling prostitution, brothel management, ID fraud, shoplifting, and drug possession. A section, tellingly titled "Victims Charged with Offences," related the astounding detail that trafficking victims had been convicted *of trafficking*. For instance, it said, "One trafficking conviction was for a 21-year-old Hungarian national who received a sentence of 12 months in a young offenders institute."[38] It likewise noted, without irony, that a "further victim has been charged with trafficking and is still progressing through the criminal justice system."[39] Clearly, police forces and the criminal justice system had categorized women as *traffickers* and as *victims* and, at times, put the same woman in both categories. This confounding process exemplifies what scholar of migration Kiril Sharapov labels "traffickersandtheirvictims," that is, a symbolic conflation merging traffickers and victims into a single criminalized class managed by the state.[40] The *Statistical Assessment* indicates how such a merger is materially borne out, primarily through the state's capture of women. The state produces material, bodily proof of trafficking, and therefore its skill at tackling trafficking, when it apprehends and categorizes people. The discursive incoherence of this process, revealed in the *Statistical Assessment,* serves the antitrafficking agenda since those captured flesh out victim

---

36. UKHTC, *Statistical Assessment*, 4.
37. UKHTC, *Statistical Assessment*, 9.
38. UKHTC, *Statistical Assessment*, 8.
39. UKHTC, *Statistical Assessment*, 15.
40. Sharapov, "'Traffickers and *Their* Victims,'" 98.

and suspect counts.[41] Yet before Pentameter 2, the UK signed the Council of Europe Convention on Action against Trafficking in Human Beings, which contains a nonpunishment provision advising states to avoid "imposing penalties on victims for their involvement in unlawful activities." As a signatory, the UK not only doled out punishments for petty crimes and activities like indoor prostitution, but it also penalized victims of trafficking officially recognized as such by the state.

Toppling the stereotype of the male East European trafficker, Pentameter 2 arrested more women than men. Most of the people arrested came from China and Southeast Asia.[42] Moreover, the majority of the people categorized as trafficked also came from China and Southeast Asia.[43] As Hua notes, during the US Progressive Era, the "derogatory usage of the term *sex slave* to indicate immigration fraud was used initially to refer to Asian women," which thus acted as "a moral appeal to block entry of Asian women."[44] The cry that women are being trafficked through immigration fraud is met by state efforts to arrest women's movement in order to protect them, or to protect the nation *from* them and their immorality. That police arrested more women than men undercut the assumption that Pentameter 2 intercepted men trafficking women. The focus on white women in antitrafficking representations obscured how nonwhite women were affected and that immigration and criminal charges were levied disproportionately against them. The epideictic rhetoric in praise of Pentameter 2 concealed the intensive policing of migrant and minority women, and men. In line with the Home Office's Coordinated Prostitution Strategy, the main reason for arrest through Pentameter 2 was brothel management, not human trafficking.[45] How did these results, restricted from the public in the *Statistical Assessment*, jive with official claims about the operation taking "tough action" against "criminal gangs"?

The *Statistical Assessment* gives a snapshot of the criminal charges, police cautions, and convictions obtained through the proactive policing of prostitution. Goal convergence under the antitrafficking agenda facilitated state crackdowns on prostitution and immigration in line with turning the UK into a hostile environment. Confirming this goal, Home Secretary Jacqui Smith stated, "Pentameter 2 is the next stage in ensuring that the UK is a hostile environment for such criminals and will send out a clear message that as a society we will not tolerate the exploitation and brutality perpetrated by these

---

41. UKHTC, *Statistical Assessment*, 2.
42. UKHTC, *Statistical Assessment*, 11.
43. UKHTC, *Statistical Assessment*, 6.
44. Hua, *Trafficking Women's Human Rights*, 37.
45. UKHTC, *Statistical Assessment*, 18.

21st century human traffickers."[46] Likewise, state agencies like the ACPO and the UKHTC promised to "take forward a diverse range of programmes to ensure that the UK becomes a hostile environment for traffickers."[47]

After winning a legal battle for access to the *Statistical Assessment*, Nick Davies wrote two news articles, which appeared in 2009 in *The Guardian*, and detailed what he called the "tide of misinformation" circulating about trafficking in the UK since the early 2000s. In one article, Davies juxtaposed the erroneous US intelligence on weapons of mass destruction that authorized invading Iraq (Operation Iraqi Freedom) with the UK intelligence on trafficking that authorized nationwide police raids (Operation Pentameter). The misinformation circuit in each instance, he argued, was "driven by political opportunists and interest groups in pursuit of an agenda."[48] In his view, anti-prostitution abolitionists used "the trafficking tale to secure their greater goal, not of regime change, but of legal change to abolish all prostitution."[49] After offering that appraisal, Davies dropped the bomb of his journalistic investigation: "after raiding 822 brothels, flats and massage parlours all over the UK, Pentameter finally convicted of trafficking a grand total of only 15 men and women."[50] Five of the ten men and all of the women were convicted without evidence that they forced anyone into prostitution. Contrary to official boasts about Pentameter, Davies concluded, "the UK's biggest ever investigation of sex trafficking failed to find a single person who had forced anybody into prostitution in spite of hundreds of raids on sex workers in a six-month campaign by government departments, specialist agencies and every police force in the country."[51] This front-page exposé begets several questions: How could such a spectacular failure be deemed a success, and how could the law secure convictions for trafficking without any evidence of force?

CRIMINALIZING ASSISTED MIGRATION: HOW TO OBTAIN TRAFFICKING CONVICTIONS

The fifteen trafficking convictions obtained under Section 57 of the Sexual Offences Act 2003 did not include the elements of force, fraud, and coercion

---

46. Jacqui Smith, Letter to the Agencies Participating in Pentameter 2.

47. Association of Chief Police Officers in Scotland, "Operation Pentameter 2 Exposes Human Trafficking."

48. Davies, "Inquiry Fails."

49. Davies, "Inquiry Fails."

50. Davies, "Inquiry Fails."

51. Davies, "Inquiry Fails."

in its definition of trafficking. Instead, trafficking for the purpose of sexual exploitation was codified as follows:

> A person commits an offence if he intentionally arranges or facilitates the arrival in the United Kingdom of another person (B) and either—
>   (a) he intends to do anything to or in respect of B, after B's arrival but in any part of the world, which if done will involve the commission of a relevant offence, or
>   (b) he believes that another person is likely to do something to or in respect of B, after B's arrival but in any part of the world, which if done will involve the commission of a relevant offence.

Section 57's language genders traffickers as men, but Pentameter 2's results did not match that rhetoric. Although the popular representation of trafficking in the UK portrayed East European men forcing East European women into sexual slavery, Section 57 assigns legal culpability to a person who arranges or facilitates the arrival of someone that "he intends" to sexually exploit or that "he believes" will be sexually exploited. Rhetorically, Section 57 links two distinct acts: (1) arranging or facilitating immigration and (2) sexual exploitation. This legal linkage turns assisted migration into the crime of human trafficking and reveals that the law figures the UK as violated by immigration it does not want. Construing irregular immigration as a *criminal* violation of the UK's sovereignty, Section 57 of the Sexual Offences Act 2003 assigns culpability for trafficking to people who did not sexually exploit anyone. This torque of legal rhetoric makes the UK out to be the real victim of trafficking by supplanting the symbolic white woman-victim with the white nation-state. Represented as though it protects women, Section 57 defends and protects the UK from the economic immigration *of women* and of anyone who assists their ability to migrate.

The UK's oscillating open- and closed-door policy toward Accession 8 citizens illustrates that immigration status fluctuates with state priorities. As a status ascribed by the state, the right to migrate interlocks with statuses like gender, race, class, sexuality, and nationality. Gender and women's studies scholar Eithne Luidhéid explains, "Illegalization (like legalization) is a *process,* not an essential quality attached to particular human bodies."[52] The process of placing people in legalized and illegalized categories is an exercise and effect of state power. Thus, Section 57 can be read as revealing that *illegal immigrant* status indicates a state's aspirations over and above a person's

---

52. Luibhéid, "Sexuality, Migration," 292.

actions. Complicating matters of categorization, an academic study of the Home Office campaigns against "illegal immigration" reported that for many people in the general public, "the distinctions between 'illegal' and 'legal,' and between asylum seeker, refugee, student, worker, resident, and sometimes between migrants and ethnic minority British-born people [are] difficult to understand."[53] The UN Special Rapporteur also found that "ethnicity continues to be deployed in the public and private sector as a proxy for legal immigration status."[54] Private individuals and civil servants, she concluded, "err on the side of excluding all but those who can easily and immediately prove that they are British or those whose White ethnicity confers upon them presumed Britishness in certain contexts."[55] While "presumed Britishness" privileged some people, negative presumptions about nonwhite and migrant women increased suspicion and scrutiny about who they were and what they were doing in Britain.

Defining trafficking as a criminal deed done by men effectively put women's migration under scrutiny to ensure they were not the victims of male traffickers. In chapter 2, I analyzed a full-page poster in the *UK Action Plan on Tackling Human Trafficking* that showed a white man, woman, and girl adorned with price tags to signify their enslaved status. The poster asked: "Did you arrange your own travel to the UK? Do you know who you are meeting in the UK? Do you know where your journey is leading in the UK?" While the text and image may appear raceless and gender neutral, the dominant discourse of women qua victims, and the condescending tone, fit with the stereotype that women were not in control of their migration and therefore needed to be questioned. That presumption enabled the prosecution, detention, and deportation of migrant women, the very population that the UK pointed to as rescue targets. Nonwhite migrant women in particular were policed and processed as "illegal migrants" even when they were also classed as trafficking victims. In this crucial way, the UK antitrafficking campaign cloaked state racism, sexism, and the targeting of economic migrants, while claiming to center victims and their rights.

Section 57 produced a punishment mechanism that impeded poor and nonwhite women's migration, especially if they had engaged in prostitution, by assigning legal culpability to anyone who helped them. Section 57 also expanded the state's carceral reach through its departure from the internationally recognized definition of trafficking. The UN's Protocol to Prevent, Suppress and Punish Trafficking in Persons defines human trafficking as

---

53. University of Warwick, "'Go Home,'" 3.
54. United Nations, *Report of the Special Rapporteur,* 16.
55. United Nations, *Report of the Special Rapporteur,* 16.

the recruitment, transportation, transfer, harbouring or receipt of persons, *by means of* the threat or use of force or other forms of coercion, of abduction, of fraud, of deception, of the abuse of power, of a position of vulnerability, or of the giving or receiving of payments or benefits to achieve the consent of a person having control over another person, for the purpose of exploitation.[56]

The definition stipulates that the threat or use of force is an essential element of trafficking into any industry. By comparison, Section 57 stretches the definition of human trafficking to include just arranging or facilitating immigration while narrowing the definition to the sex industry only. Operation Pentameter's overview explained, "There are several international protocols that cover trafficking, and indeed it is from one of these protocols—the Palermo Protocol—that we took the definition of trafficking used during Pentameter."[57] In fact, Section 57's definition of trafficking was used to levy criminal charges against people. Yet, despite the far more expansive definition, which did not require the threat or use of force, charges and convictions for trafficking in the UK were remarkably low. The government had painted a picture of a titanic network of international organized crime infiltrating British cities and towns. The Pentameters and Section 57 were made for the purpose of dealing with the large and growing scale of trafficking in the UK, but neither the police operations nor the law captured what they claimed. The chasm between legal and lay rhetoric allowed for proactive policing to be touted as a success when its results supported the opposite conclusion.

UKHTC Programme Director Grahame Maxwell admitted as much once the *Statistical Assessment* was publicly exposed. He stated, "The facts speak for themselves. I'm not trying to argue with them in any shape or form."[58] He likewise acknowledged that the scale of trafficking for sexual exploitation had been exaggerated:

What we're trying to do is to get it gently back to some reality here. It's not where you go down on every street corner in every street in Britain, and there's a trafficked individual. There are more people trafficked for labour exploitation than there are for sexual exploitation. We need to redress the balance here. People just seem to grab figures from the air.[59]

---

56. United Nations Office on Drugs and Crime, Protocol to Prevent, Suppress and Punish. My emphasis.

57. Gloucestershire Constabulary, *Pentameter Operational Overview*, 2.

58. Davies, "Inquiry Fails."

59. Davies, "Inquiry Fails."

The trouble with Maxwell's claim is the people who "seem to grab figures from the air" were the home secretary, the UKHTC head, chief constables, gold commanders, and a range of politicians and spokespeople. Officials cited dubious estimates, unanalyzed data, and sensationalistic news stories regularly when talking about trafficking. In Maxwell's previous role, he had been ACPO Lead on Trafficking and Organised Crime for Operation Pentameter. In that role, he was quoted claiming that trafficking "is happening in suburbia."[60] Fueling the dominant trafficking narrative, he further "revealed that the huge number of women trafficked into Britain was causing a fall in prices paid for prostitutes," thereby circulating the trope of foreigners economically undercutting citizens. Maxwell was then peddling a salacious story about cheap commercial sex reminiscent of the Poppy Project's *Big Brothel* report (see chapter 1).

In chapter 3, I examined the Blue Blindfold campaign, which warned Britons to be on the lookout because trafficking was happening in their towns, streets, communities, and workplaces. If Britons imagined trafficking "on every street corner in every street in Britain," it was because the government had created and circulated that image. Maxwell's avowed desire to get "back to some reality here" ignores the UKHTC's constitutive role in creating trafficking imaginary in the first place. Claiming a need to fix this false image conveniently overlooks how the UKHTC used misinformation while coordinating awareness and police campaigns. Furthermore, in Maxwell's statement, the "street corner" indexes a place conceptually tied to prostitution and petty crime, whereas Pentameter 2 mainly targeted private residences in search of serious organized crime. The *Action Plan* assured that "victims are treated first and foremost as victims of crime rather than immigration offenders," but Pentameter 2's results told a very different story.[61] The results established that Pentameter 2 failed the people it categorized as victims, led to immigration and criminal charges against migrant women, convicted people primarily for prostitution and petty crimes, and obtained a small number of trafficking convictions, but without evidence of force.

The following section focuses on the UK's National Referral Mechanism. Like proactive policing and prosecutions, the stated purpose of the NRM was to help victims of trafficking, but the trouble remained how to distinguish an innocent woman from a guilty one—a binary division that the state made and over which it again floundered.

---

60. Pallister, "Police to Launch Intelligence Unit."
61. Home Office, *UK Action Plan*, 9.

THE NATIONAL REFERRAL MECHANISM:
DIVIDE AND CATEGORIZE

All told, the UK government set up the National Referral Mechanism to meet the obligations of the Council of Europe convention, identify and assist trafficking victims, and collect victim data to ascertain the scope of trafficking. The UK ratified the convention in 2008, it came into force in the UK in 2009, and it obliged signatory states to implement countertrafficking measures and support for victims. There were immediate concerns about how it was implemented. Nine NGOs formed the Anti-Trafficking Monitoring Group (ATMG) to assess the UK's compliance with the convention because the government refused to implement regular independent monitoring of the NRM despite early indications of discretionary decisions and victims suffering as a result.[62] The ATMG issued a report, titled *Wrong Kind of Victim? One Year On: An Analysis of UK Measures to Protect Trafficked Persons,* based on a review of 390 cases, 90 interviews with antitrafficking campaigners, and publicly available information.[63] In this section, I analyze the NRM outcome statistics from 2009, as well as recorded judgments against claimants who applied for trafficking victim status.

The Council of Europe convention laid out guidelines on "Competent Authorities," which it defined as agencies likely to encounter trafficking victims, including police stations, embassies, and hospitals. The convention required that all frontline agencies in signatory states install staff trained to prevent, combat, and identify trafficking. The UK government opted to designate only two enforcement agencies, the UK Human Trafficking Centre and the UK Border Agency, as its Competent Authorities, and it divided the victim identification process along national lines. The UKHTC was tasked with assessing UK and EU/EEA nationals. The UKBA handled non-UK and non-EU/EEA nationals—or, in other words, everyone else. Arranging the infrastructure of victim identification and support in this way, the UK did not comply with but circumvented the Council of Europe convention directive to install trained staff in *all* frontline agencies. Rather than extend antitrafficking expertise across sectors like police stations, embassies, and hospitals, the

---

62. The nine organizations that initially formed the ATMG, and drafted *Wrong Kind of Victims?,* were Amnesty International UK, Anti-Slavery International, ECPAT UK (Every Child Protected Against Trafficking), the Helen Bamber Foundation, Immigration Law Practitioners Association, Kalayaan, the Poppy Project, TARA (Trafficking Awareness Raising Alliance), and UNICEF UK.

63. The Anti-Trafficking Monitoring Group's 2013 report, *In the Dock,* attested to the fact that the UK prosecuted victims of trafficking for crimes committed under duress or as a consequence of being trafficked.

UK was concentrating "competence" within two enforcement agencies. The concentrated approach stands in stark contrast to the Hostile Environment Policy's comprehensiveness. When creating hostility against "illegal migrants," the UK government tasked employers, landlords, healthcare providers, and school personnel with performing immigration checks so as to restrict access to employment, housing, healthcare, and education. Evidently, an expansive approach across sectors was feasible when fomenting hostility, but a more conservative approach was taken when protecting victims' human rights.

Making the UK Border Agency into a Competent Authority tasked enforcement officers trained to detect "illegal migrants" with also identifying trafficking victims. As a Home Affairs committee noted, NGOs were expressing concerns that "the key role to be played by the UKBA made the 'competent authority' in effect an immigration screening mechanism rather than one to identify and help victims."[64] The UKBA website expresses its purview by declaring it "is taking action against illegal migrants nationwide. Every week, our frontline officers are locating and removing migrants who flout the UK's immigration law or pose a risk to the community."[65] Visually enhancing this claim, the background shows a close-cropped image of an enforcement officer placing handcuffs on a disembodied wrist. That image conveys a message similar to that of Operation Vaken, the infamous 2013 awareness campaign that used advertising vans adorned with a close-up photograph of an enforcement officer's badge, belt, and handcuffs. On top of the image, text posed this question, "In the UK illegally?" Additionally, text in capital letters blared, "106 ARRESTS LAST WEEK IN YOUR AREA" and "GO HOME OR FACE ARREST." The UK government's offer was presented in fine print: "We can help you to return home voluntarily without fear of arrest or detention." The menacing vehicles circulated through neighborhoods in London with large immigrant populations. The visual and textual continuity between the UKBA website in 2010 and Operation Vaken in 2013 illustrates the government's investments in high-profile campaigns to frighten migrant and minority communities—profiling neighborhoods and commanding irregular migrants to deport themselves—while dismissing their fears of law and immigration enforcement. Officials routinely attributed such fears to corrupt cops "back home," denying that people had good reason to be scared as hostile environment policies were "rapidly diffusing the reach of the immigration system across sectors and society, to create what has been described as 'state racial terror.'"[66] This point tracks back to the *nationhood watch*, a concept that

---

64. House of Commons, *Trade in Human Beings*.
65. UK Border Agency, accessed October 11, 2010, www.ukba.homeoffice.gov.uk.
66. Griffiths and Yeo, "UK's Hostile Environment," 526.

I suggested in chapter 3, wherein citizens participate in a national surveillance project to maintain the value of their nation by profiling and policing others.

Thresholds of Recognition:
Claimant Nationalities and Negative Judgments

In order to receive official status as a trafficking victim, non-UK and non-EU/EEA nationals had to apply to an immigration system "characterized by restrictive policies, absurdly complex and ever-changing Immigration Rules, harsh and arbitrary decision-making, [and] criminalisation of mobility and indefinite immigration detention."[67] Receiving negative judgments from the NRM meant that those claimants could be charged with criminal and immigration offenses.

The misleading name, National Referral Mechanism, meant only referral to the UKHTC or UKBA so that these state agencies could decide whether an individual met the administrative standard to be officially identified as a victim of trafficking. It did not necessarily mean that an individual was referred to or received victim support services.[68] To the contrary, the NRM was the gatekeeper of support services. Once the NRM received a referral to evaluate someone, the process proceeded in two stages: the *reasonable grounds decision* and the *conclusive decision*. Rhetorically, the decisions took the form of threshold statements. A case manager delivering a positive reasonable grounds decision stated, "From the information available so far I believe but cannot prove" that this claimant is a victim of trafficking. For a claimant, that decision translated to a place in a safe house and up to forty-five days of "recovery and reflection" (the Council of Europe convention required a thirty-day minimum). During those days, the case was investigated further to reach the second stage and final decision. A case manager issuing a positive conclusive decision stated, "on the balance of probability it is more likely than not" that this claimant is a victim of trafficking. Conclusive decisions could not be appealed. While the NRM had lower burdens of proof than the evidentiary standards in criminal proceedings, the Anti-Trafficking Monitoring Group found that non-UK and non-EU/EEA nationals had lower rates of positive conclusive decisions than people with UK and EU/EEA citizenship. Indeed, the highest rates of positive conclusive decisions went to UK nationals but dropped the farther a claimant's country of origin was from the UK.

---

67. Griffiths and Yeo, "UK's Hostile Environment," 524.
68. Anti-Trafficking Monitoring Group, *Wrong Kind of Victim?*, 8.

Akin to the premature celebrations of Pentameter 2, officials made misleading statements about NRM results and how victims of trafficking were treated. The Home Office claimed that almost 80 percent of the people referred to the NRM received positive decisions in its first three months of operation.[69] But that claim represented only the reasonable grounds decisions, which was the first evaluative stage. To understand fully how the NRM operated, the rate of conclusive decisions needed to be known. According to the Anti-Trafficking Monitoring Group, conclusive decisions revealed a stark picture. From April to November 2009, 19 percent of NRM claimants received positive conclusive decisions, a figure that essentially flipped the Home Office claim on its head.[70] On the one hand, the Home Office's assertion that almost 80 percent of NRM referrals led to positive decisions makes it sound like the mechanism identified a lot of trafficking victims, especially without an explanation that those decisions were tentative. On the other hand, a rate of only 19 percent would raise serious questions about why most NRM referrals were rejected and why case managers at the UKHTC and UKBA concluded claimants did not meet the threshold to be recognized as victims of trafficking. As with Pentameter 2, officials hyped initial, not final, results in order to publicize what looked like an antitrafficking win.

A deeper dive into NRM outcome statistics from 2009 raises additional questions about how decisions were made and on what grounds. Recall that the UK government designated only two enforcement agencies as Competent Authorities, the UKHTC and the UKBA, with the effect of dividing victim identification along national lines. Processing UK and EU/EEA nationals, the UKHTC's positive conclusive decision rate for UK nationals was 76 percent but plummeted to 29.2 percent for EU/EEA nationals.[71] The UKBA's positive conclusive decision rate fell further, to a stunning low of 11.9 percent for non-UK and non-EU/EEA nationals.[72] Put another way, the UKHTC ruled against EU/EEA citizens at a higher rate than against UK citizens, and the UKBA, which processed people from outside the UK and EU/EEA, ruled negatively more often than the UKHTC overall. In view of the NRM outcome statistics, the Anti-Trafficking Monitoring Group argued that the mechanism to identify victims of trafficking was putting "more emphasis on the immigration status

---

69. Home Office, *Update to the UK Action Plan*, 21.

70. For that period, the UK's Competent Authorities received 477 referrals and recognized 90 of them as victims of trafficking.

71. There were some cases processed by the UKHTC that skipped the reasonable grounds stage.

72. Anti-Trafficking Monitoring Group, *Wrong Kind of Victim?*, 26.

of the presumed trafficked persons, rather than the alleged crime committed against them."[73]

For claimants, the stakes of the National Referral Mechanism were always high. If at any stage the UKHTC or the UKBA decided a claimant was not a victim of trafficking, then criminal charges, immigration charges, or both, could be brought against them. Claimants were supposed to be shielded from charges while cases were investigated, although that did not always happen in practice. If the UKBA processed the case and decided a claimant had no right to remain, then the UK could pursue deportation. But even with a positive conclusive decision, foreign nationals faced constrained options and uncertain futures. During this time, NRM claimants who received victim of trafficking status were also given three options: cooperate with police and prosecutors, accept "voluntary" repatriation, or submit an application for "leave to remain" in the UK, which the Home Office bestowed at its discretion.

Significantly, the NRM's initial outcome statistics conflicted with UK trafficking rhetoric that depicted foreign women as trafficking victims. The NRM statistics instead showed that British nationals received higher rates of positive conclusive decisions, suggesting that nationality influenced the decision-making. Foreign nationals struggled to be viewed as trafficking victims and thus to cross the UK threshold of recognition. Conclusive decisions from the two Competent Authorities did not skew toward claimants who fit the dominant narrative of transnational trafficking but toward claimants who contradicted it. The NRM doled out positive decisions to British nationals, or claimants who did not cross borders to enter the UK and did not need permission to remain in the UK. That fact reduced demand on the UK government to support and protect foreign victims of trafficking.

Measuring Victimhood: Why the National Referral Mechanism Failed Women

As Julietta Hua argues regarding the evolution of US antitrafficking legislation, "Sex trafficking is considered within the broader legal frame of sexual violence and can be read as a different kind of rape story, one that implicates illicit border crossings while hiding state violence in policing national borders."[74] In this section, I analyze several excerpts, compiled by the Anti-Trafficking Monitoring Group (ATMG), from recorded judgments, which are

---

73. Anti-Trafficking Monitoring Group, *Wrong Kind of Victim?*, 8.
74. Hua, *Trafficking Women's Human Rights*, 29.

official letters by the Competent Authorities that communicate decisions to claimants. In no uncertain terms, the ATMG contended that the NRM "creates a narrow, legally dubious, interpretation of a victim, and attaches conditions that have been proven to impede identification."[75] For instance, consent to migrate for work could be used to void the abuse a claimant experienced. Gender stereotypes also influenced whether claimants received the rights and resources tied to victim of trafficking status. Permitting a tiny percentage of people to obtain victim status, however, ultimately boosted narratives about British values and commitment to a victim-centered approach to trafficking. Professor of politics Alex Balch notes, "Even if there is supposed to be a focus on well-being for the narrow population who go through the NRM, there has been no concerted government effort to monitor or assess what happens to these individuals in the longer term."[76] Like the Pentameter operations, victim outcomes after contact with the state included deportation, disappearance, and getting lost in the system.

While outcome statistics are helpful for gleaning quantitative insights about the NRM's process of victim identification, recorded judgments reveal the precise reasons (and reasoning) that claimants received negative conclusive decisions. The recorded judgments below illustrate that, to justify their decisions, case managers mobilized stereotypes about how women ought to react to violence, and they relied on the figure of the ideal trafficking victim to discount actual women's narratives of their own experiences. The following excerpt expresses the rationale for rejecting an NRM claimant:

> You have stated that . . . your boyfriend "forced" you to have sexual intercourse with other men. You have stated that during this time you were allowed to leave the house to go to the shops. However you made no effort to escape or approach the authorities in the United Kingdom during this time. It is considered that had you been exploited as you claim you would have seized the first opportunity to escape your boyfriend.[77]

The case manager declares that the claimant is not a victim of trafficking because she did not try to escape at the first opportunity. This reasoning relies on the enduring and erroneous assumption that victims of intimate partner violence are suspect if they do not leave abusive partners. It also participates in the victim-blaming logic that doubts survivors of sexual assault if they do not flee or fight attackers. Clearly, the case manager empowered to decide

75. Anti-Trafficking Monitoring Group, *Wrong Kind of Victim?*, 10.
76. Balch, "Defeating 'Modern Slavery,'" 88.
77. Anti-Trafficking Monitoring Group, *Wrong Kind of Victim?*, 30.

the claimant's fate lacks basic understanding of intimate partner and sexual violence and the control violent partners can exert. Nevertheless, the case manager judges accounts of sexual abuse and exploitation, contending that displays of courage in an extremely abusive situation index trafficking victimhood. This negative conclusive decision finds that the claimant failed to enact a courageous display and thus failed to meet the threshold of victim of trafficking status.

By contrast, in another case, the case manager declares that the claimant is not a victim of trafficking because she was able to overcome her experience of sexual exploitation. The recorded judgment explains the negative conclusive decision in this way:

> It is considered that whilst a positive reasonable grounds decision was made on your case in 2008 a considerable amount of time has lapsed, over a year and a half in which time you have also provided supporting documentation that you have taken up employment. . . . Therefore it is considered that you have overcome the difficulties that you encountered for a short period of 3 months in 2008 and have overcome any trauma you may have suffered as a result. . . . Therefore a conclusive decision has been made that you [are] . . . not a victim of trafficking.[78]

This case manager declares that the claimant overcame the trauma because time had passed and she obtained a job. The fact that she secured employment is used against her to support the claim that she had "overcome the difficulties" and "any trauma." Her success is framed as evidence of her failure to be a trafficking victim and voids the abuse she experienced. This passage lays bare the double bind where being interpellated as an economic migrant who finds work is as perilous as being portrayed as a *benefit scrounger* who takes advantage of the UK. In the introduction to the book, I discussed how trafficked women must be rhetorically cleansed of the taint of willful migration for work due to the charge that economic migrants both live off the state and steal jobs from British workers. The xenophobic accusation depicts migrants as *benefit scroungers* and *job stealers* who cost the UK money and take what belongs to Britons. For this conclusive decision, the case manager determines that the claimant was too courageous to be a (helpless) victim and therefore fails to meet the threshold of victim of trafficking status.

Taken together, the conclusive decisions weave a trafficking tale wherein claimants must be daring enough to attempt escape but not so bold to appear

---

78. Anti-Trafficking Monitoring Group, *Wrong Kind of Victim?*, 32.

to have overcome trauma, whatever that looks like to an NRM case manager. Underlying the judgments is an expectation that women appealing to the state for recognition as victims of trafficking will be helpless or heroic at crucial moments, which illuminates the wide discretion in NRM decision-making.[79] It likewise brings to light the implicit and ill-informed metrics of victimhood that case managers applied to claimants.

Analyzing the "present-day system of human rights," philosopher Diana Tietjens Meyers compares two paradigms of victimization. First, she explicates that the pathetic victim paradigm "requires claimants to have undergone severe, documentable, humanly inflicted harm that they are not responsible for incurring."[80] Pathetic victims are beyond reproach since their "subjection to force" is so overwhelming that it vitiates their agency.[81] Second, Meyers writes that the heroic victim paradigm refers to the extremely courageous victim whose agency is "inoculated against the charge of complicity in bringing about her or his own suffering"[82] Notably, both paradigms require "morally pure" victims, excluding trafficked women who exercise agency and cannot be seen as helpless. It also excludes women migrating to escape poverty, support families, or better their lives because they are not viewed as courageous. For women who are not morally pure in relation to their migration, Meyers notes, "In Britain and the United States, they are considered 'smuggled' women; their self-narratives of attempted migration are summarily dismissed; and they receive none of the (meager) benefits that anti-trafficking laws confer on victims."[83] These paradigms help to clarify how the tropes of *freedom* and *force* are invoked in NRM decisions to measure a claimant's conduct and circumstances, dismissing the conduct as not good enough or the circumstances as not bad enough.

A final example underscores irrational grounds for dismissing an NRM claimant. In this case, a case manager rationalizes the negative conclusive decision by juxtaposing the length of the claimant's life with the length of the experience of exploitation:

> It is acknowledged that you may suffer some longer-term effects as a consequence of the experience you may have had. Ultimately, however, you have been alive for almost [. . .] years, of which [. . .] months you have spent with the previous employer. You have also spent nearly [. . .] months, more than

79. Meyers, *Victims' Stories*, 29.
80. Meyers, *Victims' Stories*, 33.
81. Meyers, *Victims' Stories*, 33.
82. Meyers, *Victims' Stories*, 36.
83. Meyers, *Victims' Stories*, 41.

twice the length of your claimed exploitation, free of any restriction on your freedom, in which time you have made friends and had access to the support and assistance provided by [. . .].[84]

The negative conclusive decisions were based on a case manager's evaluation that a claimant did not attempt escape; or a claimant secured employment; or a claimant made friends and accessed support, as well as having "been alive" for a longer time than being exploited. Of course, none of these reasons indicate that a claimant did not experience trafficking, nor should they retroactively void experiences of violence. The recorded judgments reveal that something else was judged, not the presence or absence of trafficking but the claimant herself. Did she react in a believable way to violence? Was she courageous in trying to escape? Did she heal too quickly by finding work, friends, or support? Despite what happened in the past, is she fine now? Trafficking narratives, observes anthropologist Laura María Agustín, represent victims as "passive receptacles and mute sufferers who must be saved," in a rhetorical move resembling the "colonialist operation warned against by discussions of western feminism's treatment of third world women."[85] Legal scholar Ratna Kapur avers that "access to rights and benefits is contingent on the ability of the transnational migrant to reinvent himself / herself, to become recognizable, comprehensible, and hence, non-threatening."[86] Case managers negatively judged what they saw as departures from how women should react to violence and exploitation by using their actions, or inaction, as grounds for ruling against them.

Recorded judgments imagine and depend on an ideal victim who is passive before being trafficked, courageous in attempting to escape, and helpless after being rescued. Claimants must submit testimonies in which they shift between passivity and agency at crucial moments, if they are to be believed. "Testimonial truth," Leigh Gilmore elucidates in *Tainted Witness,* "is indexed not to facts but to power."[87] This chapter and those that preceded it have unpacked how the UK trafficking agenda is indexed not to facts but to power, specifically to state power and violence.

While case managers make ontological claims about whether or not a claimant is a victim of trafficking, recorded judgments are in fact threshold statements about whether claimants reach an administrative standard established by the state. Conclusive decisions address the claimant in the second

---

84. Anti-Trafficking Monitoring Group, *Wrong Kind of Victim?,* 30. Details redacted in the report to protect the claimant's anonymity.

85. Agustín, *Sex at the Margins,* 39.

86. Kapur, "Cross Border Movements," 32.

87. Gilmore, *Tainted Witness,* 15.

person ("You"). Unlike the reasonable grounds decisions, the first person ("I") rarely speaks. Instead, the third person ("It") acknowledges, considers and, ultimately, decides whether a claimant receives victim of trafficking status. The rhetorical erasure of the adjudicating subject lends an objective tone to unappealable conclusive decisions. But this performance of objectivity masks irrational evaluations and wide discretion by making NRM judgments sound like neutral, fact-based deliberations and applications of government policy. The Anti-Trafficking Monitoring Group alleged that the NRM "appears to be relying excessively on the discretion of officials who receive minimal training to staff a mechanism supported by flawed legal guidance relating to who should be identified as victims of trafficking, and without a formal appeals process."[88] The UK government concentrated staff in only two Competent Authorities, yet the staff training and performance were deeply flawed and damaging to claimants.

In total, the Anti-Trafficking Monitoring Group detailed six substantial problems with the UK National Referral Mechanism's victim identification process. They included the (1) failure to apply the definition of trafficking correctly; (2) failure to understand what constitutes trafficking; (3) lack of familiarity with techniques to identify trafficked persons; (4) lack of training; (5) lack of coordination among agencies; and (6) management issues.[89] The group concluded, damningly, that "anti-trafficking practice in the UK is not compliant with key concepts relating to the *rule of law* itself," due to discretionary decisions and unequal applications of law.[90] Producing a hostile environment to make life miserable for "illegal migrants" was not an accidental outcome of the UK antitrafficking agenda but its stated objective. If anything, the UK demonstrated that hostility has a way of spreading, especially when stoked by the state. Although officials claimed to create a hostile environment for traffickers before expanding to target all "illegal migrants," trafficking victims suffered as a result of state-sponsored hostility, as did minority citizens who did not appear by Anglo-white standards to be British.

CONCLUSION:
STATE SOVEREIGNTY AND HUMAN MOBILITY

In this chapter, I compared official accounts of Pentameter 2 with a restricted internal report that documented its failure to find and assist trafficking

---

88. Anti-Trafficking Monitoring Group, *Wrong Kind of Victim?*, 8.

89. Anti-Trafficking Monitoring Group, *Wrong Kind of Victim?*, 33–34.

90. Anti-Trafficking Monitoring Group, *Wrong Kind of Victim?*, 6.

victims. The unprecedented proactive police operation was meant to materialize the women who populated the dominant trafficking narrative. Rather than exposing an epidemic of transnational trafficking, however, Pentameter 2 resulted in a host of criminal and immigration charges against women, particularly Asian women working in the UK sex industry. It also failed to secure convictions of anyone for forced prostitution.

Beyond the policing and prosecution side of the antitrafficking agenda, the UK set up the National Referral Mechanism in which claimants to victim status had to convince case managers that they were forced into prostitution and experienced exploitation. The emphasis was on force, lest claimants be viewed as economic or "illegal" migrants who had some agency in migrating or working in the UK. Yet when it came to UK law forbidding trafficking, the element of force fell away. To obtain a trafficking conviction, the state did not need to prove force, only that a person arranged or facilitated the migration of someone who was sexually exploited, which might mean that she later worked in the sex industry, given the looseness of this law. There are many torques in the UK antitrafficking agenda such as (1) publicizing inaccurate results of policing operations while restricting actual results from public view, (2) requiring NRM claimants to prove that they were forced while allowing the state to obtain trafficking convictions without evidence of force, and (3) concentrating staff in only two Competent Authorities to identify trafficking victims but expanding Hostile Environment Policy to subsume victims appealing to the state for protection, as well as migrants and minority citizens whose presence in the UK can be called into question.

The people negatively impacted by antitrafficking surveillance, policing, and legislation are sidelined as trafficking rhetoric centers on the figure of the East European woman forced into prostitution. Although the figure never appeared in the flesh in the numbers adduced by the state, she served as the rhetorical-material referent to mobilize state action and public sympathy. While the UK celebrates its human rights and victim-centered approach to trafficking, its coalescing of the antitrafficking and anti-immigration agendas criminalizes human mobility and curtails human rights. Its coercive categorizing of people via criminal and administrative infrastructures enacts state sovereignty *as* state violence. Thus, the anti-prostitute, anti-migrant, anti-poor, anti-Asian, and anti-Black bias and violence constituting antitrafficking and anti-immigration agendas must be made visible in order to be condemned.

CONCLUSION

The Disappearing Right to Remain

In 2018 a scandal engulfed the United Kingdom when it was publicly exposed that citizens who had immigrated from the Commonwealth Caribbean between 1948 and 1971 were being denied legal rights, losing jobs, and in some cases experiencing deportation. Known as the Windrush generation, they had resided in the UK for most of their lives, but in the first decades of the twenty-first century, officials began to claim that they had no right to remain. To prove a right to remain, members of the Windrush generation were told to demonstrate their continuous UK residence by supplying documents for every single year since 1973. This hard, and for some impossible, task caused substantial suffering, fear, and privation among people who not only had a guaranteed right to remain but had also been integral in rebuilding Britain after World War II. The targeting of the Windrush generation, and their descendants, emerged from the Conservative government's avowed Hostile Environment Policy. The approach to make life harder for "illegal migrants" expanded to target the Windrush generation.

The Hostile Environment Policy's harmful effects on different groups were "foreseeable and avoidable," according to an independent review that investigated how it pushed people into crisis.[1] As early as 2013, the Home

---

1. Williams, "Windrush Lessons Learned Review," 7. On the uses and abuses of the term "crisis" in trafficking rhetoric, see Hill, "Producing the Crisis."

Office received warnings that immigration officials had been targeting the Windrush generation and rejecting people's rights to be in Britain. Nonetheless, the government continued to restrict and cut access to daily essentials in an effort to create hardship and make life miserable for "illegal migrants." This hostile approach impacted the right to work and rent accommodation. It restricted access to marriage, banking services, healthcare, and even roads, by rejecting and revoking non-EEA nationals' licenses to drive. Government-sponsored flyers telling people to leave the UK appeared in sites used by ethnic minorities, including places of worship, shops, and community spaces. Adding to these stoppages, the hostile approach built new barriers to make it more difficult to enter the country and regularize legal status. In 2003 the UK introduced in-country residence application fees that increased dramatically starting in 2007, effectively "pricing out" poor people while generating revenue for the state.[2]

Weaving a web of immigration interventions at the level of daily life, Yeo observes that the purpose of the hostile environment is to cut immigration "by making it as unadvantageous, risky, expensive and inconvenient as possible."[3] On its face, making immigration riskier would appear to contradict the UK's pledges to tackle human trafficking, but the Hostile Environment Policy emerged from the antitrafficking plan to turn the country hostile toward traffickers. As the UK case demonstrates, hostility bleeds into other domains and feeds many agendas. Slammed as being unlawful and inhumane due to the Windrush scandal, the hostile environment materialized, by design, in a state that had championed its antitrafficking efforts as fighting inhuman criminals and uncivilized crime. Xenophobic and racist rhetorics were stretched and plasticized to capture migrants and minority citizens within national security projects, or *nationhood watch*. However, as scholar of composition and rhetoric Rebecca Dingo cautions, "feminist rhetoricians must not only examine occasion- or nation-bound rhetorics but also how arguments are transnationally networked and how neoliberal economics and neocolonial power relationships are often exigencies for particular arguments and representations."[4]

---

2. Yeo, "Briefing."

3. Yeo, "Briefing."

4. Dingo, *Networking Arguments*, 15–16. Dingo analyzes how women are situated in global economies, but her crucial point can be applied to other populations, including those under examination here.

GLOBAL NETWORKS OF STATE HOSTILITY

Starting in the 1990s, people who migrated from Commonwealth Caribbean countries to the UK were dubbed the Windrush generation after the *Empire Windrush* passenger liner, on which the first large group traveled in 1948. Due to labor shortages following World War II, the British government encouraged economic migration, but Caribbean migrants were not welcomed by everyone. As Charlotte Taylor recounts, anti-Black racism constituted a patterned response to Black people's migration. Expressed loudly by the Conservative party and press, a 1958 *Times* article conveys the tone: "Thousands of Jamaicans, Barbadians, Trinidadians, and West Africans find jobs of one kind or another in public transport. Less conspicuous is their invasion of the catering, garment, and entertainment industries."[5] Taylor comments that the metaphor describing migrants as invaders "clearly presents the targets as an extreme threat."[6] According to this view, immigration is something that the state must monitor and control, or Black people will move into labor sectors and geographic regions where they are not wanted. This enduring narrative of racial threat represents Blacks as a problem for the state and society, rather than as the solution that the government called for when labor was needed. The torque of state veneration and state violence functions, in this instance, to conceal Britain's dependence on Black labor by portraying itself as under siege by migrants who take too many jobs. Notice the double bind concocted by the racial threat narrative: it always frames Black people as thieves who either steal benefits from the state or steal jobs from white British workers. This torque also hides Britain's land and labor theft in a colonial context to represent Britain as the victim of unwanted migration which, in turn, licenses the mistreatment of Black migrants by the Anglo-white state and society.

Forgetting this history—of Commonwealth Caribbeans' citizenship and labor contributions and the systemic racism they faced—the Home Office forced members of the Windrush generation and their children to furnish extensive documentation or risk a range of repercussions, including deportation to countries that they left as young adults, or as children, or which they never knew at all. The state's demand was even more egregious because the government itself did not retain documents on the Windrush generation. The UK kept no record of those granted indefinite leave to remain after 1971

---

5. Taylor, "Representing the Windrush Generation," 14.
6. Taylor, "Representing the Windrush Generation," 14.

when its immigration policy changed.[7] Moreover, the UK failed to furnish documentation to Windrush residents affirming their settled status. If all this sounds like a messy outdated bureaucracy, for which a twenty-first-century government cannot be held responsible, a final awful fact is that in 2010 the Home Office destroyed the original landing cards of Windrush passengers. The Home Office thus knew that the Windrush generation would struggle to defend its legal status and had little recourse when seeking state records.

While the Home Office lacked a paper trail, government contractors demanded decades-worth of documents from Black Britons, some of whom were elderly and ill, and most of whom never doubted their legal status. The hostile environment frightened people from trying to clarify legal statuses because alerting the state to their situations had unpredictable and potentially life-changing consequences. The Windrush generation and its descendants had every right to remain in the UK, but the state treated Black Britons like the "illegal migrants" the Hostile Environment Policy aimed to flush out of the country. State agents unlawfully raided homes and forced people into detention but repeated warnings about discriminatory impacts and violations of the Equality Act 2010 went unheeded. Any clear-cut distinctions between legal and illegal melt into air when the state assails vulnerable populations. The Equality and Human Rights Commission concluded that the UK's aggressive approach to immigration "accelerated the impact of decades of complex policy and practice based on a history of White and Black immigrants being treated differently."[8] The evident abuse and disregard for migrants and minority citizens exposes how state violence works to reassert the claim that the UK was and remains an Anglo-white nation.

One of the harshest immigration regimes in UK history, the Hostile Environment Policy manifested through the coalescence of the antitrafficking and anti-immigration agendas. Before and after Brexit, claims about who belongs—and the material needed to substantiate belonging—mapped the UK's march toward race-based citizenship. The rhetorical-material analyses within *Trafficking Rhetoric* decelerate the torque of state veneration and state violence to make salient the UK antitrafficking agenda's moves and to wrench from its grasp the dominant narrative of "trafficked women," "illegal

---

7. The Immigration Act 1971 granted indefinite leave to remain to Commonwealth Caribbean citizens who were already in the UK. After the Act came into force in 1973, *Commonwealth citizens and their children lost the automatic right to live and work in the UK.* Henceforward, people born overseas who held British passports could only settle if they had a work permit and proof of a parent or grandparent born in the UK. The Immigration Act 1971, as precedent to the Nationality Act 1981 discussed in chapter 2, codified economic and genealogic barriers to deter nonwhite people from immigrating.

8. Equality and Human Rights Commission, "Public Sector Equality Duty," 3.

migrants," and a rational, moral state response to human threats to national identity and sovereignty. That response enabled the UK to globally network its domestic agendas via trafficking rhetoric and extraterritorial governance.

REFRAMING STATE POWER AND POLICY
THROUGH RHETORICAL-MATERIAL ANALYSIS

Trafficking Rhetoric tracked the UK antitrafficking agenda from its inception in the late 1990s to the post-Brexit era, focusing on the dominant narrative that depicted East Europeans as victims or perpetrators of trafficking. In so doing, the antitrafficking agenda worked to absolve Britain of its leading role in the transatlantic slave trade and to legitimize repressive immigration policy and the policing of vulnerable populations in the twenty-first century. The UK built its enforcement agenda on the sympathetic figure of the East European trafficked woman, constructing her as an exceptional (and acceptable) category of economic migrant. The antitrafficking agenda has been a fixture of UK governance for the past twenty years, and it both foretold and facilitated the shift from Britain managing EU immigration to negotiating its own exit from the EU, secured through claims that Brexit would restore the felt loss of national sovereignty, Britishness, and border control.

Throughout *Trafficking Rhetoric,* I perform rhetorical-material analysis to demonstrate how xenophobia and racism materialize (as) state agendas. These national enterprises, from the British Empire to Global Britain, are made manifest through human and institutional bodies in order to position the UK on the global stage. I traversed historical time and geographic scale to deconstruct a specific nation-building and rebranding enterprise that found traction under the antitrafficking agenda. Britain's age-old and active production of race via its remembering and forgetting of slavery, colonialism, and imperialism functions to deploy and disavow what it sets in motion. The chapters proceed to consider how trafficking rhetoric affords a discursive location from which to interpret the UK's changing relation to the EU, migration, and globalization. The UK government's trafficking rhetoric opened economic migrants to state violence while enabling the Home Office to claim that a hostile environment was needed to stop traffickers. The Home Office initially pointed to "21st century traffickers" as the targets of hostility, while modernizing enforcement infrastructures that subjected migrant and minority groups to unprecedented levels of state intervention. Hostility as official policy made it hard for targeted migrants and minorities to live because they were stopped, questioned, doubted, and denied. Those experiencing the full brunt of the state's Hostile Environment Policy also experienced detention and deportation.

Rhetorical-material analysis reveals the tenacity of race-baiting and gender bias in policy and how states use race and gender as proxies for managing crises. The influential book *Policing the Crisis* decoded how moral panic in Britain turned the crime of mugging into a proxy for race and legitimated the racial profiling of young Black men. Anti-Blackness anchors diverse carceral enterprises. The hostile environment rolled back material gains made by minority citizens while labor market access was closed to economic migrants in favor of policing the country. The UK at once champions multiculturalism but also avows a politics of colorblindness. Yet ongoing racial tensions appear in everyday encounters and amid global crises. When Russia invaded Ukraine in 2022, the BBC racialized Ukrainians as white to express and encourage sympathy for this group of refugees fleeing a conflict. The government spoke of Ukrainians much more compassionately than it did when discussing Syrian refugees and asylum seekers. *Trafficking Rhetoric* shows that race remains a moving target, that whiteness should be seen but not as straightforward or solid, and that racialization is the rhetorical material fabricating colonial, imperial, and neoliberal state projects.

What has *Trafficking Rhetoric* done for the discipline of rhetoric? I hope that the foregoing rhetorical-material analysis has shown what rhetorical studies can accomplish when it is activated by and deeply indebted to feminist and critical race theory; when it understands gender and race as central to state agendas tackling issues involving sex, labor, migration, and exploitation; and when it works across history and geography to trace the contours of countries coming to terms with their uncomfortable legacies, comforting lies, and power lines. This study could have been conducted in ways that left gender and race as static variables, or as asides, to the main event of "trafficking." But instead this longitudinal analysis of the UK's antitrafficking agenda situated it in a longer history of empire and larger EU context to generate insights about the ongoing entanglements of xenophobia, racism, sexism, and nationalism that made trafficking into a policy issue ripe for exploitation. Tracing the transmogrification of trafficking rhetoric as it facilitated hostile policy and border controls illuminates how a state operates to manage public memory and public feelings while concealing its own violence. By pointing to the alleged crimes of others, the UK used the abolition of the transatlantic slave trade, without attending to slavery's afterlives, to embark on a new nationalist project to define and enrich itself by controlling human freedom, labor, and movement. This book has demonstrated that studies of rhetoric can reframe a state agenda from inception to its transnational incorporation by interrogating what is the typical purview of rhetoric—terms, analogies, enthymemes, tropes, visuals, and media—as well as official estimates, policies, laws, white papers, Parliamentary debates, and prime ministers' speeches. In particular, I hope my deep dives into numeric rhetoric, law, and policy offer pathways for future studies of how a state's language materializes in and through people's lives. It is not hyperbole to say that the UK antitrafficking agenda did not affect only those classed as "trafficked women" or "traffickers" but also millions of people since it legitimized proactive police raids, closed-door immigration schemes, new criminal offences, the Hostile Environment Policy, and the historic break from the European Union.

The UK antitrafficking agenda likewise legitimized xenophobic and racist rhetoric at the critical juncture when far right ideologies embarked on a global resurgence from fringe political movements to the mainstream. While the UK is far from alone in this rightward drift, *Trafficking Rhetoric* chronicles how an agenda it seems like no one can argue against—fighting modern-day slavery—smuggles in race to morph from a rescue approach into something more insidious, that is, a binary between immigration and trafficking through which saviorhood and criminality are pronounced. This brings me to two more paths that this book foregrounds for future rhetorical-material analysis. First, racism and colonialism are inextricably linked, and they are entangled with whichever concepts are politically expedient for obfuscation, in this instance, modern-day slavery. We disregard these links at our peril, effectively cosigning on conditions in which we are caught unprepared and uncomprehending of complex political phenomena. We are seduced by easy, feel-good campaigns about helping helpless others without seeing the violent torque of state agendas. Second, and in the face of such supposedly reasonable and moral appeals, we need to build solidarity across struggles that recognize the common threads fabricating racist and anti-immigrant nationalism which roots certain bodies to land while casting others out. Third, white supremacy must be understood as expansive and explicitly transnational, in ways that harm and hail those who are peripherally white. It is incumbent on the discipline of rhetoric to engage with and reframe discourses about xenophobia, racism, sexism, colonialism, and empire, including the continuous effects of imperialist ideology and accumulation. We do this by not only focusing on the United States but by looking behind and beyond it. To this end, *Trafficking Rhetoric* charted through lines in the shared ideological inheritance of white supremacy playing out in the UK and US to this day.

The marking of some people as "good" versions of the desired category— that is, victims, migrants, and citizens—is a divisive state strategy that reappears and thrives in times of political crisis. The binary categorizations not only replicate white savior tropes but also overlay fictitious and simplistic good-versus-evil narratives onto what is, in fact, a complex and recurrent problem: the demonizing of migrant and minority groups. Colonial giving, as I wrote in the introduction, is always a form of taking. In the context of nation-building, perhaps more than elsewhere, policies emerge over time and through the circulation of kairotic rhetoric. The larger lesson in *Trafficking Rhetoric* concerns how moments of liberation come full circle, remaking the villain into the hero while securing the endurance of oppressive regimes. In times of local and global reckoning, live questions about how power works must receive sustained attention and all our analytical tools. In this way, and with this commitment, we can treat the discipline of rhetoric as a potential resource for human liberation as well as political literacy.

BIBLIOGRAPHY

Agnew, John. "Taking Back Control?: The Myth of Territorial Sovereignty and the Brexit Fiasco." *Territory, Politics, Governance* 8, no. 2 (2020): 259–72.

Agustín, Laura María. *Sex at the Margins: Migration, Labour Markets and the Rescue Industry.* London: Zed Books, 2007.

Ahmed, Sara. "Affective Economies." *Social Text* 79, vol. 22, no. 2 (2004): 117–39.

———. "Bogus." *Feminist Killjoys* (blog), October 27, 2016. https://feministkilljoys. com/2016/10/27/bogus/.

———. *Strange Encounters: Embodied Others in Post-Coloniality.* London: Routledge, 2000.

Aitkenhead, Decca. "Sarah Teather: 'I'm Angry There Are No Alternative Voices on Immigration.'" *The Guardian,* July 12, 2013. https://www.theguardian.com/theguardian/2013/jul/12/sarah-teather-angry-voices-immigration.

Allsopp, Jennifer, Nando Sigona, and Jenny Phillimore. "Poverty among Refugees and Asylum Seekers in the UK: An Evidence and Policy Review." IRiS (Institute for Research into Superdiversity) Working Paper Series No. 1/2014, University of Birmingham, UK, 2014. https://research.birmingham.ac.uk/en/publications/poverty-among-refugees-and-asylum-seekers-in-the-uk-an-evidence-a.

Anderson, Bridget, and Ben Rogaly. "Forced Labour and Migration to the UK." Study prepared by COMPAS (Centre on Migration, Policy and Society) in collaboration with the Trades Union Congress, Oxford University, UK, February 3, 2005. https://www.tuc.org.uk/research-analysis/reports/forced-labour-and-migration-uk.

Anderson, Bridget. *Us and Them? The Dangerous Politics of Immigration Control.* Oxford: Oxford University Press, 2013.

Andreas, Peter, and Kelly M. Greenhill. *Sex, Drugs, and Body Counts: The Politics of Numbers in Global Crime and Conflict.* Ithaca, NY: Cornell University Press, 2010.

Andrijasevic, Rutvica. "Beautiful Dead Bodies: Gender, Migration and Representation in Anti-Trafficking Campaigns." *Feminist Review,* no. 86 (2007): 24–44.

Anti-Trafficking Monitoring Group. *In the Dock: Examining the UK's Criminal Justice Response to Trafficking.* London, UK: Anti-Slavery International for The Anti-Trafficking Monitoring Group, 2013.

Anti-Trafficking Monitoring Group. *Wrong Kind of Victim? One Year On: An Analysis of UK Measures to Protect Trafficked Persons.* London, UK: Anti-Slavery International for The Anti-Trafficking Monitoring Group, 2010.

Asen, Robert. "Reflections on the Role of Rhetoric in Public Policy." *Rhetoric and Public Affairs* 13, no. 1 (2010): 121–43.

Association of Chief Police Officers in Scotland. "Operation Pentameter 2 Exposes Human Trafficking." News Release, July 2, 2008.

Balch, Alex. "Defeating 'Modern Slavery,' Reducing Exploitation? The Organisational and Regulatory Challenge." In *The Modern Slavery Agenda: Policy, Politics and Practice in the UK,* edited by Gary Craig, Alex Balch, Hannah Lewis, and Louise Waite, 75–96. Bristol: Policy Press, 2019.

Barad, Karen. "Diffracting Diffraction: Cutting Together-Apart." *Parallax* 20, no. 3 (July 2014): 168–87.

BBC News. "Anti-Trafficking Drive Launched." January 29, 2008. http://news.bbc.co.uk/2/hi/uk_news/7214412.stm.

BBC News. "Labour's EU Migrant Policy Was Not a Failure, Says Lord Blunkett." April 15, 2016. https://www.bbc.com/news/uk-politics-36053219.

BBC News. "Tories to Keep 'Tens of Thousands' Target." May 8, 2017. https://www.bbc.com/news/uk-politics-39840503.

BBC News. "UK Votes to LEAVE EU." https://www.bbc.com/news/politics/eu_referendum.

BBC News. "Who Are the 'A8 Countries?'" April 24, 2005. http://news.bbc.co.uk/2/hi/programmes/panorama/4479759.stm.

Berman, Jacqueline. "(Un)Popular Strangers and Crises (Un)Bounded: Discourses of Sex-Trafficking, the European Political Community and the Panicked State of the Modern State." *European Journal of International Relations* 9, no. 1 (2003): 37–86.

Bernstein, Elizabeth. *Brokered Subjects: Sex, Trafficking, and the Politics of Freedom.* Chicago: University of Chicago Press, 2019.

——. "Militarized Humanitarianism Meets Carceral Feminism: The Politics of Sex, Rights, and Freedom in Contemporary Antitrafficking Campaigns." *Signs: Journal of Women in Culture and Society* 36, no. 1 (2010): 45–71.

Best, Joel. *Damned Lies and Statistics: Untangling Numbers from the Media, Politicians, and Activists.* Berkeley: University of California Press, 2001.

Beutin, Lyndsey P. "Racialization as a Way of Seeing: The Limits of Counter-Surveillance and Police Reform." *Surveillance & Society* 15, no. 1 (2017): 5–20.

——. "There's a Trafficking Jam on the Underground Railroad: Black Abolitionist Icons and Anti-Trafficking Media." *Feminist Media Studies* (2022): 1–17.

——. *Trafficking in Antiblackness: Modern-Day Slavery, White Indemnity, and Racial Justice.* Durham, NC: Duke University Press, 2023.

Bindel, Julie. "Revealed: The Truth about Brothels." *The Guardian,* September 9, 2008. https://www.theguardian.com/lifeandstyle/2008/sep/10/women.socialexclusion.

Bindel, Julie, and Helen Atkins. *Big Brothel: A Survey of the Off-Street Sex Industry in London.* London, UK: The Poppy Project / Eaves Housing for Women, 2008.

Blair, J. Anthony. "The Rhetoric of Visual Arguments." In *Defining Visual Rhetorics,* edited by Charles A. Hill and Marguerite Helmers, 41–61. Mahwah, NJ: Lawrence Erlbaum Associates, 2004.

Blair, Tony. "Slavery: Bicentenary of the Abolition." HL Deb (November 28, 2006). Vol. 687, col. 89WS. https://hansard.parliament.uk/Lords/2006-11-28/debates/061128101000011/SlaveryBicentenaryOfTheAbolition.

Blanchette, Thaddeus Gregory, and Ana Paula da Silva. "On Bullshit and the Trafficking of Women: Moral Entrepreneurs and the Invention of Trafficking in Persons in Brazil." *Dialectical Anthropology,* no. 36 (2012): 107–25.

Bland, Archie. "Black Lives Matter Sculpture of Jen Reid Removed from Colston Plinth." *The Guardian,* July 16, 2020. https://www.theguardian.com/world/2020/jul/16/black-lives-matter-sculpture-of-jen-reid-removed-colston--bristol.

———. "Edward Colston Statue Replaced by Sculpture of Black Lives Matter Protester Jen Reid." *The Guardian,* July 15, 2020. https://www.theguardian.com/world/2020/jul/15/edward-colston-statue-replaced-by-sculpture-of-black-lives-matter-protester.

Blastland, Michael, and Andrew Dilnot. *The Numbers Game: The Commonsense Guide to Understanding Numbers in the News, in Politics, and in Life.* New York: Gotham Books, 2009.

Blomfield, Paul. "The Government's Silence on Immigration Tightens Its Blindfold on Brexit." *New Statesman,* December 4, 2018. https://www.newstatesman.com/politics/2018/12/government-s-silence-immigration-tightens-its-blindfold-brexit.

Bonilla-Silva, Eduardo. "The Invisible Weight of Whiteness: The Racial Grammar of Everyday Life in Contemporary America." *Ethnic and Racial Studies* 35, no. 2 (2010): 173–94.

Braidotti, Rosi. "On Becoming Europeans." In *Women Migrants from East to West: Gender, Mobility and Belonging in Contemporary Europe,* edited by Luisa Passerini, Dawn Lyon, Enrica Capussotti, and Ioanna Laliotou, 23–44. New York: Berghahn Books, 2007.

Bristow, Edward. *Prostitution and Prejudice: The Jewish Fight against White Slavery, 1870–1939.* New York: Schocken, 1983.

Brooks-Gordon, Belinda. "Red Mist Obscures Red Light Statistics." *The Guardian,* April 3, 2009. https://www.theguardian.com/commentisfree/2009/apr/03/prostitution-humantrafficking.

Brown, Gordon. "Managed Migration and Earned Citizenship." Speech delivered at the Camden Centre, London, February 20, 2008.

Browne, Stephen H. "Remembering Crispus Attucks: Race, Rhetoric, and the Politics of Commemoration." *Quarterly Journal of Speech* 85, no. 2 (1999): 169–87.

Chapkis, Wendy. "Trafficking, Migration, and the Law: Protecting Innocents, Punishing Immigrants." *Gender & Society* 17, no. 6 (2003): 923–37.

Chávez, Karma R. *The Borders of AIDS: Race, Quarantine, and Resistance.* Seattle: University of Washington Press, 2021.

———. *Queer Migration Politics: Activist Rhetoric and Coalitional Possibilities.* Urbana: University of Illinois Press, 2013.

Chuang, Janie A. "Rescuing Trafficking from Ideological Capture: Prostitution Reform and Anti-Trafficking Law and Policy." *University of Pennsylvania Law Review* 158, no. 6 (2010): 1655–728.

Cisneros, J. David. "Contaminated Communities: The Metaphor of 'Immigrant as Pollutant' in Media Representations of Immigration." *Rhetoric & Public Affairs* 11, no. 4 (2008): 569–601.

———. *The Border Crossed Us: Rhetorics of Borders, Citizenship, and Latina/o Identity.* Tuscaloosa: University of Alabama Press, 2013.

Clarke, Amy. "Recognising British Bodies: The Significance of Race and Whiteness in 'Post-Racial' Britain." *Sociological Research Online* 28, no. 1 (2021): 1–17.

Cobain, Ian. "Albanians Take Over Organised Crime." *The Times,* November 26, 2002. https://www.thetimes.co.uk/article/albanians-take-over-organised-crime-5jwwggkfplj.

Cohen, Stanley. *Folk Devils and Moral Panics: The Creation of the Mods and Rockers.* London: MacGibbon and Kee, 1972.

Council of Europe Convention on Action against Trafficking in Human Beings, Council of Europe Treaty Series—No. 197, Warsaw, 16.V.2005.

Councilor, KC. "Feeding the Body Politic: Metaphors of Digestion in Progressive Era US Immigration Discourse." *Communication and Critical/Cultural Studies* 14, no. 2 (2017): 139–57.

Davies, Nick. "Inquiry Fails to Find Single Trafficker Who Forced Anybody into Prostitution." *The Guardian,* October 20, 2009. https://www.theguardian.com/uk/2009/oct/20/government-trafficking-enquiry-fails#:~:text=The%20UK's%20biggest%20ever%20investigation,police%20force%20in%20the%20country.

———. "Prostitution and Trafficking: The Anatomy of a Moral Panic." *The Guardian,* October 19, 2009. https://www.theguardian.com/uk/2009/oct/20/trafficking-numbers-women-exaggerated.

DeChaine, D. Robert, ed. *Border Rhetorics: Citizenship and Identity on the US-Mexico Frontier.* Tuscaloosa: University of Alabama Press, 2012.

Devereux, Cecily. "'The Maiden Tribute' and the Rise of the White Slave in the Nineteenth Century: The Making of an Imperial Construct." *Victorian Review* 26, no. 2 (2001): 1–23.

Dickson, Sandra. *Sex in the City: Mapping Commercial Sex across London.* London, UK: The Poppy Project / Eaves Housing for Women, 2004.

Dingo, Rebecca. *Networking Arguments: Rhetoric, Transnational Feminism, and Public Policy Writing.* Pittsburgh: University of Pittsburgh Press, 2012.

Dixon, Hugo. "Just Say No to a 'Blindfold Brexit.'" *Politico,* September 19, 2018. Last updated April 19, 2019. https://www.politico.eu/article/just-say-no-to-a-blindfold-brexit-theresa-may-chequers-plan/.

Doezema, Jo. "Loose Women or Lost Women?: The Re-Emergence of the Myth of White Slavery in Contemporary Discourses of Trafficking in Women." *Gender Issues* 18, no. 1 (2000): 23–50.

———. *Sex Slaves and Discourse Masters: The Construction of Trafficking.* London: Zed Books, 2010.

Donovan, Brian. *White Slavery Crusades: Race, Gender, and Anti-Vice Activism, 1887–1917.* Urbana: University of Illinois Press, 2005.

Dubourg, Richard, and Stephen Prichard, eds. *The Impact of Organised Crime in the UK: Revenues and Economic and Social Costs.* London: Home Office, n.d.

Dubourg, Richard, Sameen Farouk, Linda Miller, and Stephen Prichard. "People Trafficking for Sexual Exploitation." In *The Impact of Organised Crime in the UK: Revenues and Economic and Social Costs,* edited by Richard Dubourg, Sameen Farouk, Linda Miller, and Stephen Prichard, 14–22. London: Home Office, n.d.

Dustmann, Christian, Maria Casanova, Michael Fertig, Ian Preston, and Christoph M. Schmidt. *The Impact of EU Enlargement on Migration Flows.* Home Office Online Report 25/03. London: Research Development and Statistics Directorate / Home Office, 2003.

El-Tayeb, Fatima. *European Others: Queering Ethnicity in Postnational Europe.* Minneapolis: University of Minnesota Press, 2011.

Emelife, Aindrea. "'Hope Flows through This Statue': Marc Quinn on Replacing Colston with Jen Reid, a Black Lives Matter Protester." *The Guardian,* July 15, 2020. https://www.theguardian.com/artanddesign/2020/jul/15/marc-quinn-statue-colston-jen-reid-black-lives-matter-bristol.

Equality and Human Rights Commission. "Public Sector Equality Duty." Last updated February 22, 2023. https://www.equalityhumanrights.com/en/advice-and-guidance/public-sector-equality-duty.

Faulkner, Elizabeth A. "40.3 Million Slaves: Challenging the Hypocrisy of Modern Slavery Statistics." *Open Democracy,* October 31, 2017. https://www.opendemocracy.net/en/beyond-trafficking-and-slavery/403-million-slaves-challenging-hypocrisy-of-modern-slavery-statistics/.

Fedina, Lisa. "Use and Misuse of Research in Books on Sex Trafficking: Implications for Interdisciplinary Researchers, Practitioners, and Advocates." *Trauma, Violence, and Abuse* 16, no. 2 (2015): 188–98.

Feingold, David A. "Trafficking in Numbers: The Social Construction of Human Trafficking Data." In *Sex, Drugs, and Body Counts: The Politics of Numbers in Global Crime and Conflict,* edited by Peter Andreas and Kelly M. Greenhill, 46–74. Ithaca, NY: Cornell University Press, 2010.

Farrell, Thomas B. "Sizing Things Up: Colloquial Reflection as Practical Wisdom." *Argumentation,* no. 12 (1998): 1–14.

Finnegan, Cara A. "The Naturalistic Enthymeme and Visual Argument: Photographic Representation in the 'Skull Controversy.'" *Argumentation and Advocacy* 37, no. 3 (2001): 133–49.

FitzGerald, Sharron A. "Vulnerable Geographies: Human Trafficking, Immigration and Border Control in the UK and Beyond." *Gender, Place & Culture* 23, no. 2 (2016): 181–97.

Fixmer-Oraiz, Natalie. *Homeland Maternity: US Security Culture and the New Reproductive Regime.* Urbana: University of Illinois Press, 2019.

Flores, Lisa A. *Deportable and Disposable: Public Rhetoric and the Making of the "Illegal" Immigrant.* University Park: Pennsylvania State University Press, 2021.

Forkert, Kirsten, Emma Jackson, and Hannah Jones. "Whose Feelings Count? Performance Politics, Emotion and Government Immigration Control." In *Emotional States: Sites and Spaces of Affective Governance,* edited by Eleanor Jupp, Jessica Pykett, and Fiona M. Smith, 177–90. London: Routledge, 2016.

Foucault, Michel. *Discipline and Punish: The Birth of the Prison.* Translated by Alan Sheridan. New York: Penguin Books, 1991.

Fox, Jon E., Laura Moroşanu, and Eszter Szilassy. "The Racialization of the New European Migration to the UK." *Sociology* 46, no. 4 (2012): 680–95.

Garner, Steve. *Whiteness: An Introduction.* London: Routledge, 2007.

Gayle, Damian. "How Bristol Came Out in Support of the Colston Four." *The Guardian,* January 5, 2022.

Gephardt, Katarina. *The Idea of Europe in British Travel Narratives, 1789–1914.* Routledge, 2016.

Gloucestershire Constabulary. *Pentameter Operational Overview.* July 2006. Quedgeley, Gloucester.

Gloucestershire Constabulary. *Chief Constable's Annual Report 2008/2009.* Quedgeley, Gloucester.

Gomez, Logan Rae. "Temporal Containment and the Singularity of Anti-Blackness: Saying Her Name in and across Time." *Rhetoric Society Quarterly* 51, no. 3 (2021): 182–92.

Goode, Erich, and Nachman Ben-Yahuda. *Moral Panics: The Social Construction of Deviance.* Hoboken, NJ: Wiley Blackwell, 1994.

Griffiths, Melanie, and Colin Yeo. "The UK's Hostile Environment: Deputising Immigration Control." *Critical Social Policy* 41, no. 4 (2021): 521–44.

Grittner, Frederick K. *White Slavery: Myth, Ideology and American Law.* New York: Garland Press, 1990.

Hall, Catherine. "Britain 2007, Problematising Histories." In *Imagining Transatlantic Slavery,* edited by Cora Kaplan and John Oldfield, 191–201. Basingstoke: Palgrave Macmillan, 2010.

Hall, Stuart. "Racism and Reaction." In *Five Views on Multi-Racial Britain: Talks on Race Relations Broadcast by BBC TV,* 23–35. 2nd ed. London: Commission for Racial Equality, 1978. https://eric.ed.gov/?id=ED186570.

Hall, Stuart, Chas Critcher, Tony Jefferson, John Clarke, and Brian Roberts. *Policing the Crisis: Mugging, the State and Law and Order.* 2nd ed. London: Bloomsbury Publishing, 2013.

Hamilton, Douglas. "Representing Slavery in British Museums: The Challenges of 2007." In *Imagining Transatlantic Slavery,* edited by Cora Kaplan and John Oldfield, 127–44. Basingstoke: Palgrave Macmillan, 2010.

Harris, Leslie J. "Rhetorical Mobilities and the City: The White Slavery Controversy and Racialized Protection of Women in the US." *Quarterly Journal of Speech* 104, no. 1 (2018): 22–46.

———. *The Rhetoric of White Slavery and the Making of National Identity.* East Lansing: Michigan State University Press, 2023.

Haynes, Dina Francesca. "(Not) Found Chained to a Bed in a Brothel: Conceptual, Procedural, and Legal Failures to Fulfill the Promise of the Trafficking Victims Protection Act." *Georgetown Immigration Law Journal,* no. 21 (2007): 377–81.

Helmers, Marguerite, and Charles A. Hill. Introduction to *Defining Visual Rhetorics,* edited by Charles A. Hill and Marguerite Helmers, 1–23. Mahwah, NJ: Lawrence Erlbaum Associates, 2004.

Hesford, Wendy S. *Spectacular Rhetorics: Human Rights Visions, Recognitions, Feminisms.* Durham, NC: Duke University Press, 2011.

———. *Violent Exceptions: Children's Human Rights and Humanitarian Rhetorics.* Columbus: The Ohio State University Press, 2021.

Heynen, Robert, and Emily van der Meulen. "Anti-Trafficking Saviors: Celebrity, Slavery, and Branded Activism." *Crime, Media, Culture* 18, no. 2 (2022): 301–23.

Hill, Amelia. "'Hostile Environment': The Hardline Home Office Policy Tearing Families Apart." *The Guardian,* November 28, 2017. https://www.theguardian.com/uk-news/2017/nov/28/hostile-environment-the-hardline-home-office-policy-tearing-families-apart.

Hill, Annie. "Demanding Victims: The Sympathetic Shift in British Prostitution Policy." In *Negotiating Sex Work: Unintended Consequences of Policy and Activism,* edited by Carisa R. Showden and Samantha Majic, 77–97. Minneapolis: University of Minnesota Press, 2014.

———. "How to Stage a Raid: Police, Media and the Master Narrative of Trafficking." *Anti-Trafficking Review,* no. 7 (2016): 39–55.

———. "Producing the Crisis: Human Trafficking and Humanitarian Interventions." *Women's Studies in Communication* 41, no. 4 (2018): 315–19.

———. "The Rhetoric of Modern-Day Slavery: Analogical Links and Historical Kinks in the United Kingdom's Anti-Trafficking Plan." *Philosophia* 7, no. 2 (2017): 241–60.

Hodkinson, Stuart N., Hannah Lewis, Louise Waite, and Peter Dwyer. "Fighting or Fuelling Forced Labour? The Modern Slavery Act 2015, Irregular Migrants and the Vulnerabilising Role of the UK's Hostile Environment." *Critical Social Policy* 41, no. 1 (2021): 68–90.

Home Office. *A Coordinated Prostitution Strategy and a Summary of Responses to Paying the Price*. London: Home Office, 2006.

Home Office. *Human Trafficking: The Government's Strategy*. London: HM Government, 2011.

Home Office. *UK Action Plan on Tackling Human Trafficking*. London: Stationery Office, 2007.

Home Office. *Update to the UK Action Plan on Tackling Human Trafficking*. London: Stationery Office, 2009.

House of Commons. *The Trade in Human Beings: Human Trafficking in the UK*. Home Affairs Committee, Sixth Report of Session 2008–09. London: Stationery Office, 2009.

Hua, Julietta. *Trafficking Women's Human Rights*. Minneapolis: University of Minnesota Press, 2011.

Jones, Hannah, et al. *Go Home? The Politics of Immigration Controversies*. Manchester, UK: Manchester University Press, 2017.

Kafer, Alison. *Feminist Queer Crip*. Bloomington: Indiana University Press, 2013.

Kapur, Ratna. "Cross Border Movements and the Law: Renegotiating the Boundaries of Difference." In *Trafficking and Prostitution Reconsidered: New Perspectives on Migration, Sex Work, and Human Rights,* edited by Kamala Kempadoo, Jyoti Sanghera, and Bandana Pattanaik, 25–42. Boulder, CO: Paradigm Publishers, 2005.

Kelly, Liz, and Linda Regan. *Stopping Traffic: Exploring the Extent of, and Responses to, Trafficking in Women for Sexual Exploitation in the UK,* edited by Carole F. Willis. Police Research Series, Paper 125. London: Home Office Research, Development, and Statistics Directorate, 2000.

Kempadoo, Kamala. "The Modern-Day White (Wo)Man's Burden: Trends in Anti-Trafficking and Anti-Slavery Campaigns." *Journal of Human Trafficking* 1, no. 1 (2015): 8–20.

Kempadoo, Kamala, and Elena Shih. "Rethinking the Field from Anti-Racist and Decolonial Perspectives." In *White Supremacy, Racism and the Coloniality of Anti-Trafficking,* edited by Kamala Kempadoo and Elena Shih, 1–13. New York: Routledge, 2023.

Kundnani, Arun. *The End of Tolerance: Racism in 21st Century Britain*. London: Pluto Press, 2007.

Laite, Julia. *Common Prostitutes and Ordinary Citizens: Commercial Sex in London, 1885–1960*. Basingstoke: Palgrave Macmillan, 2011.

Levine, Philippa. *Prostitution, Race, and Politics: Policing Venereal Disease in the British Empire*. New York: Routledge, 2003.

Luibhéid, Eithne. "Sexuality, Migration, and the Shifting Line between Legal and Illegal Status." *GLQ: A Journal of Lesbian and Gay Studies* 14, nos. 2–3 (2008): 289–315.

Mahdavi, Pardis, and Christine Sargent. "Questioning the Discursive Construction of Trafficking and Forced Labor in the United Arab Emirates." *Journal of Middle East Women's Studies* 7, no. 3 (Fall 2011): 6–35.

Maynard, Robyn. "Do Black Sex Workers' Lives Matter? Whitewashed Anti-Slavery, Racial Justice, and Abolition." In *Red Light Labour: Sex Work Regulation, Agency, and Resistance,* edited by Elya M. Durisin, Emily van der Meulen, and Chris Bruckert, 281–92. Vancouver: University of British Columbia Press, 2018.

McDowell, Linda. "Old and New European Economic Migrants: Whiteness and Managed Migration Policies." *Journal of Ethnic and Migration Studies* 35, no. 1 (2009): 19–36.

Merry, Sally Engle. *The Seductions of Quantification: Measuring Human Rights, Gender Violence, and Sex Trafficking*. Chicago: University of Chicago Press, 2016.

Meyers, Diana Tietjens. *Victims' Stories and the Advancement of Human Rights*. New York: Oxford University Press, 2016.

Mohanty, Chandra. "Under Western Eyes: Feminist Scholarship and Colonial Discourses." *Feminist Review*, no. 30 (1988): 3–28.

Musto, Jennifer Lynne. "What's in a Name?: Conflations and Contradictions in Contemporary US Discourses of Human Trafficking." *Women's Studies International Forum* 32, no. 4 (2009): 281–87.

National Archives. "Blue Blindfold—Don't Close Your Eyes to Human Trafficking." Archived on April 6, 2010. https://webarchive.nationalarchives.gov.uk/ukgwa/20100406123243/http://www.soca.gov.uk/about-soca/about-the-ukhtc/your-help-campaigns?tmpl=component&print=1&page=.

Niblett, Robin. "The Sovereignty Argument for Brexit Is a Myth." *Newsweek*, May 10, 2016. https://www.newsweek.com/brexit-eu-sovereignty-argument-myth-457816.

O'Brien, Erin. *Challenging the Human Trafficking Narrative: Victims, Villains, and Heroes.* New York: Routledge, 2018.

O'Connell Davidson, Julia. *Modern Slavery: The Margins of Freedom.* Basingstoke: Palgrave Macmillan, 2015.

———. "Will the Real Sex Slave Please Stand Up?" *Feminist Review*, no. 83 (2006): 4–22.

Oliviero, Katie E. "Sensational Nation and the Minutemen: Gendered Citizenship and Moral Vulnerabilities." *Signs: Journal of Women in Culture and Society* 36, no. 3 (2011): 679–706.

Olusoga, David. "The History of British Slave Ownership Has Been Buried: Now Its Scale Can Be Revealed." *The Guardian*, July 11, 2015. https://www.theguardian.com/world/2015/jul/12/british-history-slavery-buried-scale-revealed.

Pallister, David. "Police to Launch Intelligence Unit to Target Human Trafficking." *The Guardian*, June 22, 2006. https://www.theguardian.com/news/2006/jun/22/crime.immigrationandasylum.

Parsons, Timothy H. *The British Imperial Century, 1815–1914: A World Historical Perspective.* Lanham, MD: Rowman and Littlefield, 1999.

Parvulescu, Anca. *The Traffic in Women's Work: East European Migration and the Making of Europe.* Chicago: University of Chicago Press, 2014.

Perrigo, Billy. "'Get Brexit Done.' The Three Words That Helped Boris Johnson Win Britain's 2019 Election." *Time*, December 13, 2019. https://time.com/5749478/get-brexit-done-slogan-uk-election/.

Phoenix, Joanna. *Making Sense of Prostitution.* Basingstoke: Palgrave Macmillan, 1999.

Poppy Project. *POPPY Project's Comments in Response to 'Academics' Response to Bindel & Atkins' "Big Brothel" Report.* London: The Poppy Project / Eaves Housing for Women, n.d. https://image.guardian.co.uk/sys-files/Education/documents/2008/10/07/poppyresponse.pdf.

Pratt, Mary Louise. *Imperial Eyes: Travel Writing and Transculturation.* New York: Routledge, 2007.

Ringeisen-Biardeaud, Juliette. "'Let's Take Back Control': Brexit and the Debate on Sovereignty." *French Journal of British Studies* 22, no. 2 (2017): 1–17.

Ritchie, Marnie. "Feeling for the State: Affective Labor and Anti-Terrorism Training in US Hotels." *Communication and Critical/Cultural Studies* 12, no. 2 (2015): 179–97.

Ryan, Michael. *Philosophy of Marriage in Its Social, Moral and Physical Relations.* London: John Churchill, 1837.

Sanders, Teela, Jane Pitcher, Rosie Campbell, Belinda Brooks-Gordon, and Maggie O'Neil. *An Academic Response to "Big Brothel."* 2008. Accessed via uknswp.org.

Schwarz, Corinne, and Trevor Grizzell. "Trafficking Spectacle: Affect and State Power in Operation Cross Country X." *Frontiers: A Journal of Women Studies* 41, no. 2 (2020): 57–81.

Serhan, Yasmeen. "In a Bid to 'Take Back Control,' Britain Lost It." *The Atlantic,* March 28, 2019. https://www.theatlantic.com/international/archive/2019/03/brexit-britain-control-may-eu/585940/.

Sharapov, Kiril. "'Traffickers and *Their* Victims': Anti-Trafficking Policy in the United Kingdom." *Critical Sociology* 43, no. 1 (2017): 91–111.

Sharma, Nandita. "Anti-Trafficking Rhetoric and the Making of Global Apartheid." *NWSA Journal* 17, no. 3 (2005): 88–111.

———. "Travel Agency: A Critique of Anti-Trafficking Campaigns." *Refuge: Canada's Journal on Refugees* 21, no. 3 (2003): 53–65.

Shih, Elena. "The Fantasy of Spotting Human Trafficking: Training Spectacles in Racist Surveillance." *Wagadu: A Journal of Transnational Women's and Gender Studies* 22, no. 1 (2021): 105–37.

Siddique, Haroon, and Clea Skopeliti. "BLM Protesters Topple Statue of Bristol Slave Trader Edward Colston." *The Guardian,* June 7, 2020. https://www.theguardian.com/uk-news/2020/jun/07/blm-protesters-topple-statue-of-bristol-slave-trader-edward-colston.

Smith, Jacqui. Letter to the Agencies Participating in Pentameter 2. In "UK—Trafficking—Project Pentameter 2—Targets Sale of Women & Children," Women's UN Report Network, July 7, 2008. https://wunrn.com/2008/07/uk-trafficking-project-pentameter-2-targets-sale-of-women-children.

Smith, Joanna. "Feds Launch Human Trafficking Awareness Campaign." *Toronto Star,* September 7, 2010. https://www.thestar.com/news/canada/feds-launch-human-trafficking-awareness-campaign/article_31da00b5-9bc9-5931-a2a8-1c936bca1255.html.

Sternberg, Joseph C. "Europe's 'Nationalism' Turns Out to Be Local: Le Pen, Salvini, and Brexit All Have an Appeal Limited to Particular Regions of Their Respective Countries." *Wall Street Journal,* May 9, 2019. https://www.wsj.com/articles/europes-nationalism-turns-out-to-be-local-11557442852.

Stratton, Allegra. "Labour: Now It's Kind of Blue." *The Guardian,* April 24, 2009. https://www.theguardian.com/politics/blog/2009/apr/24/blue-labour-conservative-socialism.

Suchland, Jennifer. *Economies of Violence: Transnational Feminism, Postsocialism, and the Politics of Sex Trafficking.* Durham, NC: Duke University Press, 2015.

Swingen, Abigail L. *Competing Visions of Empire: Labor, Slavery, and the Origins of the British Atlantic Empire.* New Haven, CT: Yale University Press, 2015.

Taylor, Charlotte. "Representing the Windrush Generation: Metaphor in Discourses Then and Now." *Critical Discourse Studies* 17, no. 1 (2020): 1–21.

Townsend, Mark. "Home Office Used Charity Data Map to Deport Rough Sleepers." *The Observer,* August 19, 2017. https://www.theguardian.com/uk-news/2017/aug/19/home-office-secret-emails-data-homeless-eu-nationals.

———. "'Sex Slaves' Win Cash in Landmark Legal Deal." *The Observer,* December 16, 2007. https://www.theguardian.com/uk/2007/dec/16/immigration.ukcrime.

———. "Sex-Trafficked Women's Charity Poppy Project in Danger as Funding Withdrawn." *The Guardian,* April 16, 2011. https://www.theguardian.com/society/2011/apr/17/prostitution-human-trafficking#:~:text=The%20withdrawal%20of%20funding%20means,to%20the%20organisation's%20case%20workers.

Townsend, Mark, and Aaron Walawalkar. "Home Office Revives Plan to Deport Non-UK Rough Sleepers." *The Observer,* March 27, 2021. https://www.theguardian.com/uk-news/2021/mar/27/home-office-revives-plan-to-deport-non-uk-rough-sleepers.

The Independent. "Trafficking Crackdown Frees 170 Victims," July 2, 2008. https://www.independent.co.uk/news/uk/crime/trafficking-crackdown-frees-170-victims-858714.html.

Travis, Alan. "Officials Launch Drive to Seek Out Illegal Migrants at Work." *The Guardian,* May 15, 2007. https://www.theguardian.com/uk/2007/may/16/immigration. immigrationandpublicservices.

———. "Sex Trafficking Victims Rescued by Police May Face Deportation." *The Guardian,* October 3, 2007. https://www.theguardian.com/uk/2007/oct/04/ukcrime.prisonsandprobation.

Travis, Alan, and Andrew Sparrow. "New Law to Criminalize Men Who Pay for Sex with Trafficked Women." *The Guardian,* November 19, 2008. https://www.theguardian.com/society/2008/nov/19/prostitution-justice#:~:text=The%20new%20offence%20will%20include,knew%20it%20at%20the%20time.

Tyler, Imogen. *Revolting Subjects: Social Abjection and Resistance in Neoliberal Britain.* New York: Zed Books, 2013.

UK Border Agency. *Enforcement Instructions and Guidance: Immigration Offences and Breaches.* London, May 2010.

UK Border Agency. *Victims of Trafficking: Guidance for Frontline Staff.* London, October 2010.

UK Human Trafficking Centre. *Statistical Assessment of Victims Recovered and Suspects Arrested during the Operational Phase of Operation Pentameter 2.* March 2009.

United Nations Human Rights Council. *Report of the Special Rapporteur on Contemporary Forms of Racism, Racial Discrimination, Xenophobia and Related Intolerance.* May 27, 2019. https://www.ohchr.org/en/documents/country-reports/ahrc4154add2-visit-united-kingdom-great-britain-and-northern-ireland.

United Nations Office on Drugs and Crime. Protocol to Prevent, Suppress and Punish Trafficking in Persons, Especially Women and Children, Supplementing the United Nations Convention against Transnational Organized Crime. 55 / 25, November 15, 2000. https://www.ohchr.org/en/instruments-mechanisms/instruments/protocol-prevent-suppress-and-punish-trafficking-persons.

United Nations Office on Drugs and Crime. United Nations Convention against Organized Transnational Crime and the Protocols Thereto. 55 / 25, November 15, 2000. https://www.unodc.org/unodc/en/organized-crime/intro/UNTOC.html.

US Department of Homeland Security. "About Blue Campaign." https://www.dhs.gov/blue-campaign/about-blue-campaign.

US State Department. *Trafficking in Persons Report.* 2009. https://2009-2017.state.gov/j/tip/rls/tiprpt/2009/123130.htm.

University of Warwick. "Go Home: Mapping the Unfolding Controversy of Home Office Immigration Campaigns." End of Project Findings, June 2015. https://mappingimmigrationcontroversy.com/.

Virdee, Satnam, and Brendan McGeever. "Racism, Crisis, Brexit." *Ethnic and Racial Studies* 41, no. 10 (2018): 1802–19.

Walkowitz, Judith R. *Prostitution and Victorian Society: Women, Class, and the State.* Cambridge: Cambridge University Press, 1980.

Walters, William. "Secure Borders, Safe Haven, Domopolitics." *Citizenship Studies* 8, no. 3 (2004): 237–60.

Waterton, Emma, and Ross Wilson. "Talking the Talk: Policy, Popular and Media Responses to the Bicentenary of the Abolition of the Slave Trade Using the 'Abolition Discourse.'" *Discourse and Society* 20, no. 3 (2009): 381–99.

Webber, Frances. "On the Creation of the UK's 'Hostile Environment.'" *Race and Class* 60, no. 4 (2019): 76–87.

Williams, Rachel. "British-Born Teenagers Being Trafficked for Sexual Exploitation within the UK." *The Guardian,* July 3, 2008. https://www.theguardian.com/society/2008/jul/03/childprotection.internationalcrime#:~:text=Teenage%20girls%20born%20in%20Britain,other%20towns%20for%20further%20exploitation.

Williams, Wendy. "Windrush Lesson Learned Review." March 2020. https://www.gov.uk/government/publications/windrush-lessons-learned-review.

Wood, Marcus. "Significant Silence: Where Was Slave Agency in the Popular Imagery of 2007?" In *Imagining Transatlantic Slavery,* edited by Cora Kaplan and John Oldfield. Basingstoke: Palgrave Macmillan, 2010: 162–90.

Yea, Sallie. "The Politics of Evidence, Data and Research in Anti-Trafficking Work." *Anti-Trafficking Review,* no. 8 (2017): 1–13.

Yeo, Colin. "Briefing: What Is the Hostile Environment, Where Does It Come From, Who Does It Affect?" *Free Movement,* May 1, 2018. https://freemovement.org.uk/briefing-what-is-the-hostile-environment-where-does-it-come-from-who-does-it-affect/.

Young, Jock. *The Drugtakers.* London: MacGibbon and Kee, 1971.

Young, Lola. "The Truth in Chains." *The Guardian,* March 14, 2007. https://www.theguardian.com/uk/2007/mar/15/race.past.

INDEX

NEW DIRECTIONS IN RHETORIC AND MATERIALITY

WENDY S. HESFORD, CHRISTA TESTON, AND SHUI-YIN SHARON YAM, SERIES EDITORS

Current conversations about rhetoric signal ongoing attentiveness to and critical appraisal of material-discursive phenomena. New Directions in Rhetoric and Materiality provides a forum for responding to and extending such conversations, but also asks that books published in the series attend to social events of consequence unfolding around the world—such as violence based on misinformation, continued police brutality, immigration legislation and migration crises, and more. The series therefore seeks to amplify books that examine rhetoric's relationship to materiality while also confronting material-rhetorical forces of oppression, power imbalances, and differential vulnerabilities.

www.ingramcontent.com/pod-product-compliance
Lightning Source LLC
Chambersburg PA
CBHW020356270326
41926CB00007B/451